Moses Smith

Plain Truths about Stock Speculation.

How to Avoid Losses in Wall Street...

Moses Smith

Plain Truths about Stock Speculation.
How to Avoid Losses in Wall Street...

ISBN/EAN: 9783337241742

Printed in Europe, USA, Canada, Australia, Japan

Cover: Foto ©Suzi / pixelio.de

More available books at **www.hansebooks.com**

PLAIN TRUTHS

About Stock Speculation.

HOW TO AVOID LOSSES

IN

WALL STREET.

WITH

VISITORS' DIRECTORY

IN

AND AROUND NEW YORK.

PREFACE.

————

THIS work contains plain truths, plainly told, of the dangers and folly of dealing on margins. To the uninitiated it is a revelation and exposure of the trickery and sharp practices which prevail in the marts of speculation. It is a warning to keep out of Wall Street ; and any man or woman who, after reading this book, goes there, will do so with their eyes wide open to the traps and pitfalls which will surround them. It tells of the only true and generally safe way to deal in stocks and make money. To the investor it is an invaluable guide. All of which is respectfully submitted, *pro bono publico*, by

THE AUTHOR.

INDEX.

STOCK SPECULATION.

CHAPTER I.

WALL STREET GLOSSARY.

THIS chapter is to explain the technical terms used in stock speculation.

Bulls are optimists. They buy stocks for an advance, and " go long of the market."

Bears are pessimists. They sell stocks for a decline, and " go short of the market."

Money is made or lost with equal facility, whether stocks go up or go down. It all depends on being on the right side of the market.

Bulls are not always bulls; neither are bears always bears. They are bulls at one time, bears at another, as occasion seems to serve. Some, while bearish for a decline to enable them to buy cheap, are always bulls on moral principle—that it is wrong to sell property they do not possess.

A bear must borrow stock from day to day to keep good his deliveries of stock he sold, but did not have. This is done for him by his broker.

A " corner or squeeze " is when it is difficult or impossible for bears to borrow stock to make a delivery on their contracts. Hence they are forced to buy in the stock they sold, but did not have, at whatever price the bulls may choose to ask.

"Loaning rates" are often exacted for stock loans when there is a large short interest outstanding, and stocks are made scarce in the "loan crowd." The rate may be but 39 cents-per day for the loan of 100 shares, in addition to the market value of the stock wanted, or it may be $\frac{1}{8}$ or $12.50 per day. When the bears are cornered and pressed to the wall, the rate may be from 1 per cent. or $100 to 5 per cent. or $500 for one day's loan of each 100 shares of stock.

The "loan crowd" are the brokers who congregate by themselves in the board-room with stocks to loan.

Cliques and pools are combinations of capitalists formed to control the specialties in which they are interested. Bull pools boom the market for a rise or hold values steady against the attacks of the bears. Bear pools operate to destroy values to scare timid holders of long stock into liquidation and to bring about a decline to enable them to cover their shorts at a big profit.

Deliveries of stock bought "regular" must be made before a certain time on the following business day. In default complaint is made to the Chairman of the Exchange, who buys in the stock "under the rule," and charges all differences to the delinquent.

On Options—"Buyer 3-30 or 60," or "seller 3-30 or 60," either party has 3-30 or 60 days, as the case may be, to call for or tender the stock at the price named.

Oversold is when the bears have overreached themselves and sold more stock than there is afloat.

Overloaded is when the bulls have bought more stock than they can take and pay for.

Investors are those who buy and pay for their stocks for the dividends. They aim to buy low in the hope ultimately of selling out at a big profit, in addition to the income.

Tape speculators are those who operate for catch-penny profits from day to day on margins. They are as regular habitues of the offices as the brokers themselves.

Averaging—If a bull buys 100 or more shares of stock at, say 90, and it goes down ten points, he will aim to buy more at 80. His stock then averages him 85, plus commissions. If the stock goes to 85¼, he can get out just even, provided he has no interest to pay for carrying. All the stock goes above 85¼ will be his profit. With the bear the case is reversed. If he sells stock short at 80, and it goes up, he will aim to sell more at 90, to average down.

Margins—The banker-broker usually requires $1,000, or 10 per cent., to be put up as security for each 100 shares he buys for customers. With this

margin as a basis, the banker will buy 100 shares
of stock that costs anywhere up to $10,000 or
$15,000, and "carry" it for his customers.   He
will credit the customer with interest on the $1,000
margin he put up and debit him with legal interest
on all the stock cost above the margin, and, in
addition, charge him with whatever extra rate of
interest he has to pay in time of monetary stringency.   Thus, if 100 shares of stock cost $10,000,
the customer would be credited with interest on
$1,000 and charged interest on $10,000 until the
deal was closed.   In a steady market some brokers
will carry stock for customers on a 5 per cent.
margin, or even less.   If a customer gets badly
"left," the broker will demand more margin to be
put up; failing in that, the broker will take good
care to close out the deal in time to save his commissions and interest.

Commissions are ⅛ per cent., or $12.50 to buy;
the same to sell, making the cost of a turn in 100
shares $25.

Call and Time Loans—Although the legal rate
of interest in New York is 6 per cent., since the
repeal of the Usury Law, relating to call loans, by
the Act of 1882, the banks can charge any higher
rate they choose when money is scarce.   From the
1st of January, 1884, up to the first months of
1886, owing to the great plethora of money, call
loans were obtained from day to day on good collateral at from 1 to 2½ per cent. per annum.   At

one time the banks had about $65,000,000 reserve above the 25 per cent. legal requirements, and a total capital of over $160,000,000, that almost went begging for employment. During all this time the brokers could obtain all the money they required from day to day at from 1 to 3 per cent. by hypothecating the stock they carried for customers as collateral, or they could obtain time loans at 3 to 4 per cent. per annum ; and during all this time they charged customers 6 per cent., thus making fat profits on both commissions and interest.

Points—In one sense prices are said to have advanced or declined one or more points, meaning prices had gone up or down one or more per cent., or one or more dollars per share. In another sense, a man has the point that the market or a certain stock will advance or decline. He has the point or a pointer on the movements of the market.

"The Street" means the exchanges and the brokerage offices within the speculative arena on Wall and the neighboring streets.

"Cats and Dogs," also called the Fancies, are non-dividend paying stocks, which have small intrinsic value, except to be inflated like "South Sea Bubbles," to the profit of the bulls or sold short and raided down in the interest of the bears.

Liquidation in Wall Street is peculiar. If a man loaded down with obligations should sell his stocks on a rising market, and make anywhere from one to ten, fifteen or more dollars a share, that would not be regarded as liquidation, even though he used the proceeds to pay his debts. But if, through the influence of fear, when distrust prevails, he should order his stocks sold at a loss of one, ten or fifteen dollars a share, that would be Simon Pure liquidation, and is the kind the bears always work and hope for.

Washes or Wash Sales are purely fictitious, and are made by connivance between two brokers, or two sets of brokers, the one to bid up or bid down stocks, the other to appear to buy or sell the stock. Resort is had to " washes " to attain various ends at little or no expense. A wash may be had to get a quotation for an inactive stock reported, or it may be had to sustain prices when the market is in a condition of stagnation and apathy, and values tend to waste away under the offerings of tired holders. Big bulls loaded with stocks may have overstayed their market, then recourse is often had to washes to give the market an appearance of firmness and activity while they are feeding out their stocks to the fools who are tempted to make real purchases. Bears also wash values down to shake out long stock, and enable them to cover their shorts at a good profit, or to buy in a good line of long stock at low prices, preparatory to a boom. In a moral point of view, the system of stock washing is as villainous as the methods of the bunco steerer. Outsiders must pay $25 on each turn buying and selling 100 shares. Brokers can have their orders executed by other brokers for $2 and $4 for buying, and the same for selling 100 shares. Brokers can buy or sell for themselves free ; hence, two sets of brokers having the same axe to grind on certain lines of stocks can wash prices up or down free, gratis, for nothing.

Room Traders—One class of brokers execute orders for their customers on commission, and do not speculate themselves. Others operate both for themselves and on account for their customers. Room traders speculate solely for their own account, and the market is what they make it when the manipulating pools have no movements on hand.

Stock Privileges are contracts entitling the holder to receive or deliver a certain stock at any time within a period limited, usually to 30 or 60 days. The buyer pays a fixed price for the contract, and his entire liability in the transaction is limited to that amount.

A Put entitles the holder to put or deliver the stock to the maker of the contract at any time within the life of the privilege. A stock may be worth 50 at market. The put may read 46 per cent. The buyer pays, say $150 for the contract. The stock must decline to below 46 before the buyer can recover any part of the price he paid for his privilege. At $44\frac{1}{2}$ he stands to recover his

$150, and all the stock declines below 44½ will be his profit, if he puts his stock at the right time.

A Call is the reverse of a put, and entitles the holder to demand the delivery of the stock to him at the price named. If the stock is worth 50 at market, the call may read 54 per cent. If the contract cost $150, the stock must advance to 55½ before he can recover the purchase money. All it goes above 55½ will be his profit.

A Spread is both a put and a call. If the stock is 50 at market and the put price is 46, and the call price is 54, and he paid $150 for the double privilege, the stock must decline to 44½ or advance to 55½ before he can recover his purchase money. All the stock goes below 44½ or above 55½ will be his profit.

A Straddle is also a double privilege, and usually costs much more than a put, call, or spread. The price named in the straddle is the current market price, say 50. The privilege may cost $500. The stock must advance above 55 or decline below 45 before he can recover any part of his purchase money. If the stock goes up to 60 or down to 40 he can get back his $500, and all the price goes above 60 or below 40 will be his profit. It all depends, however, on his closing out the deal when he has a profit in sight within the life of the contract; otherwise, if he waits too long his profits may disappear like the birds of the night.

Stock Privileges are not recognized by the rules of the Stock Exchange. But the makers are usually capitalists abundantly able to make good their obligations.

Speculators buy privileges as a protection against wide fluctuations in prices. Bears buy calls and sell stocks short against them for profitable turns. Bulls buy puts and go long against them, and if " badly left " they are protected to a certain extent against losses.

The central point of stock speculation, on which the whole business revolves, is the fact that on the purchase or sale of 100 shares of stock, each fluctuation of 1 per cent., up or down, represents a gain, or loss, of $100.

The broker is simply an agent acting for his principal. The ultimate responsibility is always with the customer. He must take the risk, not only of the failure of his own broker, but of losses occasioned by the fraud or failure of others with whom his broker has made contracts for him in good faith.

The most potent and indispensable adjuncts to stock speculation are the Stock Indicators, or " Tickers," and the " News Tape." These are electrical printing machines by which quotations from the Stock Exchange, and news and rumors of good or ill omen, gathered at the news agencies, are instantly flashed over the wires and reeled off, in print, in all the brokers' offices, as well as in the bar-rooms and restaurants where speculators congregate.

There is also a manifold news service, being letter-press copies on tissue paper, or slips run through lightning printing machines and distributed by messengers as fast as news is gathered.

It is shrewdly suspected, if not an actual fact, that these agencies are, upon occasion, under the subsidy of the big manipulators of the market, who have news, rumors and roorbacks calculated to lead, or mislead, ground out to order, to further their interests.

Wall Street is the center of financial and political news wired from all over the country, or flashed by cable from all over the world. The death of a man great in politics or finance, big failures, defalcations, defaults in interest on railway bonds, etc., carry dismay into the ranks of the bulls, and correspondingly elate the bears. Called United States Bonds by the Secretary of the Treasury, names and time of winning horses at Saratoga, Brighton, Monmouth Park and Cedarhurst, and the progress of the international yacht races were all noted.

The difference between New York and London time is five hours. When it is 10 o'clock A. M. in the latter place it is 5 o'clock A. M. in the former. Several times a day quotations of American stocks in London are received. By figuring the difference in the rate of exchange it is readily ascertained whether stocks are higher or lower there than in New York. The strength of one market is reflected by that of the other.

There are a half dozen or more Wall Street dailies, devoted to the interests of speculation. They give stock news and gossip from the bull or bear standpoint, and essay to forecast the movements of the market. But it is hit or miss; if they hit right two or three days in succession, they are always prophets after the event.

The morning or evening papers all give more or less extended market reports and gossip, and pander to the instinct for stock gambling. Some papers employ paid financial writers. " In and Out of Wall Street," by " Rigolo," was formerly a feature in Monday's edition of the New York *Sun*, and were eagerly devoured. He was said to have received $100 a column.

The " Wall Street " column in Saturday's *Evening Telegram* has more interest to a certain class of readers than the instructive cartoons of De Grimm, the artist.

CHAPTER II.

THE AMERICAN BOURSE.

And rumor (she's a famous liar, yet
'Tis wonderful how easy we believe her)
Had whispered he was rich, and all he met
    "In Wall street nodded, smiled and tipped the beaver ; "
        All, from Mr. Gelston, the collector,
        Down to the broker and bank director.

A few brief years passed over, and his rank
    Among the worthies of that street was fixed ;
He had become director of a bank,
    And six insurance offices, and mixed
        Familiarly, as one among his peers,
        With grocers, dry goods merchants, auctioneers.

Brokers of all grades—stock and pawn—and Jews
    Of all religions, who at noonday form,
On 'Change, that brotherhood the moral muse
    Delights in, where the heart is pure and warm,
        And each exerts his intellectual force
        To cheat his neighbor—legally, of course.
                    —FITZ GREENE HALLECK.

WITH the exception of a long narrow hallway to
the board room, the New York Stock Exchange is not on Wall Street at all.   It is on Broad
and New Streets, near the centre of the block
between Wall Street and Exchange Place. It
consists of two buildings of entirely opposite

character, yet joined together and thrown into one. On Broad Street it is five stories high, with a white marble front and portico. The "long room" is on the first floor, and the "bond room" is on the floor above. In the basement are coat rooms, and safe deposit vaults of solid masonry.

The "board room" is a substantial brick building with stone trimmings and a slated gable roof. It is on, and runs parallel with New Street, has long windows with stout iron shutters, and is like and yet unlike a country church. The height of the room from floor to ceiling is equal to the height of the four story and high stoop building adjoining it on the south. It is in this room that more money is made and lost by insiders and more fortunes of the outside public are swamped than in any other business in America.

To become a member of the Stock Exchange a man must buy a "seat," then he must apply for membership, and if not black-balled, he is admitted and becomes a full fledged broker. "Seats" are a myth so far as the board room is concerned. It is an open floor with not sittings enough for more than 50 or 60 of the 1,100 brokers. Originally a membership cost $100. As the number of brokers and the volume of business grew and increased, the price of a seat also increased, until now a seat is worth from $25,000 to $30,000, and the highest price ever paid was $35,000, a year or two since.

On the wall back of the north gallery of the present board room is the legend, " Erected MDCCXCII " (1792); this, however, can refer only to the time when the stock brokerage business was started in a small way, for the present Broad Street building was finished and occupied in 1865 and the building on New Street in 1880.

The Board of Brokers, as it was called before it claimed to be entitled The New York Stock Exchange, commenced business with eighteen members, and met in a room over what was known as Jauncey's stables, in Wall Street. James W. Bleeker, David Clarkson, Samuel Ward, James G. King and G. G. Howland were among the leading members. The Board met at 11 A. M., and adjourned at 12. Each broker carried a small book in which the prices current and transactions of the day were recorded. There was but little to record; a few shares of bank stock and a few insurance stocks were the securities dealt in. Railroads were not then invented.

At what was then No. 42 Wall Street were the offices of Prime, Ward & Sands, afterwards Prime, Ward & King; John Ward and Co., Vermilye & Co., Nevins & Townsend, and others. Time was not as valuable as now, and instead of the short, jerky cry of "a thousand more," and "take 'em," as is uttered at present in the height of business a hundred times a minute, Mr. King, perhaps, would appear on the steps of his office with deliberation and dignity announce that he had some United States Bank stock to sell, naming the number of shares and price. A few words of consultation among the crowd of half a dozen listeners and an offer would be made, somewhat in these terms: " Mr. King, we understand the price named to be the lowest acceptable, sir." To which Mr. King would reply: " The very lowest, sir." " In that case we will take the lot, sir, at the pleasure of the buyer in three days," and the transaction was concluded.

Mr. Samuel Ward was the father of the late Sam Ward, the disciple of Savarin, the poet, the uncle of Marion Crawford, the " Roi du Vestibule," as Blaine called him. Sam Ward was educated abroad, and was thought to possess extraordinary ability as a mathematician. On his return from Europe he was taken as a partner in the house of Prime, Ward & King, and an amusing anecdote was told as illustrating his ignorance of Wall Street matters. He entered the office of a prominent broker and asked what the effect would be of a purchase of 20,000 shares of a certain stock, and was told it would be to advance the price several per cent. Then said Mr. Ward: " You may buy for me 20,000 shares and sell them out again at the advance, sending me your check for my profit," ignoring the fact that as buying would advance, so selling would depress the price, and other things being equal, no profit accrued.

One of the prominent old time brokers was Mr. William H. Hayes, who afterwards became President of the Bank of the State of New York. His father, Jacob Hayes, was famous as the first, last and only Lord High Constable of the City of New York, who, before the time of Police Commissioners, Captains and Patrolmen, ruled the disorderly elements of the city.

The Stock Exchange had various abiding places until it located permanently in its present quarters. At first it transacted its business on the sidewalk, then in rooms over a stable, and from there moved into the old Warren Building. In 1842 it became located in the rotunda of the Merchants' Exchange, which is now the Custom House. It remained there until between 1850 and 1860, when it removed into Exchange Place, and from there to William Street.

In 1879 the Exchange purchased the premises which it now occupies on New Street and erected the present board-room building, which has a frontage of 150 feet on New Street. The cost of the lots was $375,000 and included a strip running through to Broad Street 90 feet wide and 170 feet deep through the block.

Boston, Philadelphia and Baltimore each have their Stock Exchanges, but the business done in them bears no comparison, in volume and magnitude, to that done in the great whirlpool of Gotham.

A smart sharp-witted young man, who can but just command the means to buy a seat in the Exchange, is in luck. His seat is a fortune in itself. Possessing a seat he can form a partnership with some man who can furnish all the money needed to found a commission brokerage business, on a basis of a division of the profits. The broker's membership is an offset against his partner's capital. The latter is the banker, who runs the office, while the broker is on the floor of the Exchange to receive and execute orders sent to him.

Large capitalists and speculative railway directors, who deal in stocks by the tens of thousands of shares, buy seats solely for the immense saving in brokerage commissions. As brokers themselves, they can have their orders executed by other brokers for from $2 to $4 to buy or sell 100 shares, where as outsiders they would have to pay $12.50, or $25 on each turn in 100 shares.

Hazing is practiced on the admission of new members. On his first entrance to the board room he will be set upon, his $10 silk hat may be knocked off and kicked into complete collapse ; his $40 coat may be torn down the back; he will be lucky if the seat of his breeches don't give way in the melee : he may be hoisted on a table and spun around on his sit-down until drunk with confusion ; he may be thrown to the floor, back up, while some rollicking broker grabs his ankles like the handles of a wheelbarrow, and makes him paddle around the room on his hands. He will finally make his escape looking as though he had been through a cage of wild animals. From thenceforth he will be treated as a full fledged member, and will doubtless take a hand in putting the next fellow through the mill.

The personnel of the Exchange are a splendid lot of fellows, so debonair, with a chic and esprit de corps scarcely matched by any other class of business men anywhere. They are bon-vivants in high living ; connoisseurs in wines, generally good looking, dressed in the latest fashion, quick, keen-witted in a trade or to see the point of a joke. Jolly, frisky and sportive as so many colts, they are willing to pay a good price for their fun. One time an organ grinder, his wife and baby were looking in through the New Street door. They were seized on and dragged into the room greatly to their terror. One broker took the organ and ground out the music, another took the baby and showed it around, a third passed around his hat. When the fun was over, organ and baby were restored and the hat emptied of about $45 into the hands of the lately demoralized Italians, who left grinning all over at their good luck. Sometimes fun will be made of people in the gallery, and once in awhile the brokers get overmatched in an unexpected quarter, and their fun recoils like a boomer-ang. A spruce-looking darkey leaned over the gallery rail one afternoon viewing the crowd below. Some of the members on the floor below spied him and yelled, " Yah ! yah ! " and began singing, " Hoe dat Corn." The darkey nodded approval, and fishing a nickel from his pocket, tossed it down to them. The singers' voices were stilled and the rest of the crowd on the floor howled.

Brokers are of all classes. Sunday-school super-intendents, teachers, exhorters, deacons, church wardens, laymen, society dilettante and gam-blers.

Originally Stock Exchanges were organized to make a market to distribute public securities among the people by absolute purchase and sale. On first principles they were a power for good in promoting great public enterprises, in opening up new regions for settlement, in developing the re-sources of the country, and in aiding to provide new sources of industry in the building of rail-roads, canals, steamships, and in bringing to the surface, for public use, the mineral wealth of gold, silver, copper, iron and coal.

Ostensibly the rules of the Exchange hedge around its members a rigid code of honor and a high standard of commercial excellence against sharp practices or unfair advantage between brok-ers, or brokers and customers. With the increase of membership and the enormous growth of business, abuses crept in, in stock deals on margins, in short sales of what one does not own and has no moral right to sell, in stock watering, stock washing and the whole train of evils, which, for many years, have made the New York Stock Exchange, in very truth, the greatest gambling hell in America.

All brokers are not room traders and disseminators of fictions to mislead. Many are bulls from principle, first, last and all the time. They are there, however, to make money, and will execute orders to sell short stock as readily as to buy for the long account. They leave the morality of the thing to the conscience of their customers.

A class of them are millionaire bankers, brokers, room traders, operators and manipulators of the market all rolled into one. They inflate or depress values. They give out false pointers to rope in innocent people. They resort to tricks that would out Herod Mephistopheles and fictions that would discount Gulliver and Baron Munchausen. They inflate values only to sell out at the top to the suckers they can draw into their net. They go short and improvise fierce raids to destroy values by bidding down prices on washes. They doubtless subsidize the rumor mills, to fill the minds of their victims with fear and distrust, that prices have no bottom, and induce them to throw over their stocks through terror of greater losses.

Often almost the whole class of brokers are used

as the tools to promote the same business methods, and through whom the same ends are attained by unscrupulous, powerful and ruthless outside capitalists.

On the grand theatre of the world nations fight battles on the gory field of Mars. Parties wage contests in the bloodless realms of politics, with the axiom that " to the victors belong the spoils." As it was in the Trojan war, for the possession of a voluptuous woman, just so it is in the arena of speculative finance for the almighty dollar. It is on the principle that they who can win by stratagem and superior craft are entitled to the booty.

A modern poet, with the rich imagery of a Homer, would find an unlimited field for imaginative fancy in an epic depicting the battles between the bulls and the bears. The great capitalists and manipulators of the stock market and their following, as bull and bear heroes, would offset Achilles, Patroclus, Ajax and the Myrmidon bands against great Hector, Sarpedon, Æneas and the Trojan hosts. Figuratively, the flash of the electric lightning over telegraph and telephone wires with news of good or evil omen would be the descent of Juno, Minerva and Pallas like meteors from Olympus with commands from Jove to turn the financial scale for bull to drag bear or bear to drag bull at the tail of his chariot.

"WALL STREET'S LAMB.

Wall Street had a little Lamb,
  It's fleece was very thick ;
At every turn the market took
  The Lamb was sure to stick.

It followed up and followed down
  With every rise and fall,
Preferring to be done quite brown
  Rather than not at all.

The eager brokers cleaned him out,
  But still he lingered near,
And waited patiently about
  To get his margins clear.

The brokers got them, clear and clean,
  For they were " out of meat ; "
But still he waited, starved and lean,
  And hung about " the street."

" What makes the Lamb love Wall Street so ? "
  The curious rounders cry.
Why, Wall Street loves the Lamb, you know,
  And wool is scarce and high. "

CHAPTER III.

TYPICAL BANKERS AND BROKERS.

YOUR true banker is one who conducts the operations of National, State and savings banks, and guards the money you have deposited with him with the fidelity of a bull dog. We are not treating of this class in this chapter.

It is the bastard bankers who furnish facilities for gambling operations on margins and who make their profits out of commissions, interest and shaves. They are the class we mean.

Usually their names stand more or less high on 'Change, for they have money, and " money makes the mare go " everywhere. In Wall Street, of all places, " nothing succeeds like success."

In true legitimate business every one gets, or expects to get, value for value given. Too often these bankers influence and lead customers into ventures for the mere sake of gain to themselves.

Customers put up money and go in. If they make a profit, they win a bet for which they give no value to the other fellow. If they lose, the other fellow gets a value for which he gives no equivalent. Win or lose, the bankers get their commissions and interest, and too often the customers have nothing to show in return. All this is contrary to Divine law to give full value for value received.

In Wall Street, with the exception of interest on railway bonds and dividends on investment stocks, every dollar made in speculation is made by one man, or set of men, at the loss of some other man or set of men.

It is out of this business that the commission bankers wax fat and grow rich at the expense of their victims. Morally there is no difference whether one makes his commissions on a stock gamble, or on pool selling at a horse-race.

In stock transactions at least ninety per cent. of all the deals are on margins. It is the same in oil, grain, provisions and cotton futures.

Stock bankers and brokers have their offices on Exchange Place, on Nassau, Broad, Wall, Broadway and New Streets. Some have branch offices up town in or near the great hotels, or in other cities more or less distant, all connected with the down town offices by private wires.

Some of the most powerful men in the market had their offices on Broadway overlooking Trinity Churchyard, so quiet—so beautiful. "Only man is vile." But "dead men tell no tales" of the sharp practices of the conscienceless money sharks.

The offices are often fitted up with elegant opulence. Rich carpets, rugs, soft luxurious furniture, tickers, news tape, price lists, stock manuals, the City Directory and the commercial agency books of R. G. Dun & Co. and Bradstreet, and the financial publications, greet the eye.

Everything is inviting. "Walk into my parlor, says the spider to the fly." The bankers are all smiles. Their hands and voices are soft and purring. Their politeness is of the kid-glove order.

What can we do for you to-day, Mr. Fitznoodle?

We have the point that moonshine stock is good for a big rise. We advise buying that for a turn. We can buy you 100 shares for each $1,000 margin you put up. Our commissions are one-eighth to buy, one-eighth to sell, only $25 on each turn of 100 shares. The interest to "carry" won't amount to much. One of our customers made a two per cent. profit yesterday in twenty minutes. Did you ever make money like that?

Your order. Yes, ah, thanks! Make yourself at home. All the conveniences of our office are at your disposal. In effect, the talk is often about as above, with variations, sometimes more so.

So Fitz becomes a tape speculator and hanger on of the office. Small successes soon lead to infatuation. If a gain of one or two points appears, the banker or an office attendant will admonish him: "Always take profits in sight." So Fitz is got out only to be got in again.

How disinterested (?), but inwardly the banker chuckles. He has made $25 commissions on a turn in 100 shares, or $250 on a turn in 1,000 shares, as the case may be. With plenty of customers the bankers make money as slick as grease. No risks and losses to them.

Chilling frosts fill Fitz with fear, but if he is a fat gander to pick, the banker or his clerks will encourage him. " We never advise to take a loss, stocks go up and stocks go down ; hold on, the market will turn and you will come out all right !" The banker don't know his own head from his tail, how the bug will jump.

If stocks go down to within two or three per cent. of exhausting his margin, Fitz will get a hint to put up more money; failing to do that the banker will take precious good care to close him out in time to save his commissions and interest.

In the great depression of 1883–4, when stocks had a fall of from 30 to 100 per cent., some bankers were opinionated bulls all through it. Their advice was, " Hold on, the market will turn and you will come out all right."

Such advice, while valuable in a moderately fluctuating market, was ruin to those who followed their lead through the great bear raids and the long depression.

Take Union Pacific stock as an illustration. In 1882 its highest price was 119$\frac{3}{4}$. In 1883 its highest was 104$\frac{3}{4}$. In 1884 its highest was 84$\frac{5}{8}$, and its lowest price was $28 per share. Many other stocks declined in the same ratio.

In such a time the true policy was to " run," and run quickly. In some instances bull houses

themselves went down in the crash, and customers by hundreds and thousands were carried under
through their leadership.

It was the bear houses and their pessimist customers who made money out of the misplaced
confidence of the optimists.

Bankers and brokers are there to make money.
They do not cheat or rob *a l'outrance.* But they
do get into their customers all the same, for commissions through the damnable influences they
exert.

With all their soft ways and smooth palaver,
more or less of them are wolves in sheep's clothing. Many are adepts in the role of good Lord,
good devil, and hard drinkers, out of business
hours.

Their chief god is Mammon. In the time of
Aaron they would have bowed down in worship
of the " Golden Calf," in hopes of getting away
with it to melt up into shekels.

Many have been in the business from twenty
to fifty years. In that time what multitudes of
victims have been lured into their nets and dragged
down from comfort to penury !

Not a few are worth from half a million to millions of dollars, still their greed is unsatisfied.
Some advertise widely (in effect) for new victims
to come to the shambles for the periodical sheep
shearings.

Often, often their customers are cast in losses

of hundreds and thousands of dollars on each 100 shares, but that does not signify to these soft-voiced, smooth-purring and polite rogues.

Banker-brokers value investors in the dividend payers, according to the extent of their purchases, but these buy for the income and only bring grist to their mills at long intervals. Far above them the brokers value the margin customers, whom they can manipulate in and out, and milk for frequent commissions and interest on stocks they carry for them.

Commissions are not the only perquisites to the stock houses, for, in times when money is a drug, they can borrow at from 1 to 4 per cent. to carry stocks for customers, and charge them 6 per cent., pocketing the difference as profit. They have other opportunities to make money on loaning rates and for voting rights when customers are napping.

No gambling system was ever more cunningly devised to mulct the unwary than that of the stock market. The bankers know this. Still they reach out for new fish to their net, like the tentacles of an octopus; still they bait the hook for new victims, and paint bright argosies of good things to come on the wings of Æolus.

Customers by the hundreds and thousands have revolved around the outer circles of the maelstrom, and many of them have disappeared to penury in the vortex. Still the evanescent mirage of wealth is held out and the same damnable influences are brought to bear to get people in and out for those fat little plums of $25 on a turn in each 100 shares.

Bankers and brokers all know that the concomitants of speculative finance are jugglery, legerdemain, adroit trickery, wheels within wheels, marked cards, loaded dice, secret manipulation, false pretenses, unfounded rumors of great good or dire misfortune—that it is a deception by those who make and unmake the market, which in almost any other business would bring its perpetrators within the pale of criminal law. Yet they are, to all intents and purposes, ropers-in and stool pigeons to the oligarchy of millionaire commercial gamblers, who concoct ever-recurring Emma Mine, Credit Mobilier, and other schemes, to allure the public, and eventually scoop the innocents by practices on a par with the methods of the bunco steerer and the sawdust swindler.

Were this villainous system of purchases on margins, and short selling of other people's propperty squelched by law, such practices could not obtain. This whole species of gambling, both at the exchanges and the bucket shops, would be wiped out.

Millionaires and capitalists, who could afford to pay for their stocks, would be left to prey upon each other, and it would be "dog eat dog" between them.

Enormous fortunes of tens and hundreds of millions could not be rolled up in a decade by practices which are nothing short of a species of robbery.

As it is, the bankers' and brokers' offices, almost without exception, offer unlimited facilities for margin gambling in long or short stock. The masses are lured in, and the few hundred or few thousand dollars they possess is all risked on a game of chance, and a very one-sided game at that.

In the bucket shops the deals are anywhere from 5 shares to 1,000 shares at a single quotation on a one per cent. margin or upwards.

Within the past year or so the legal authorities and the police of New York and Brooklyn have been stirred to unwonted activity in breaking up pool selling on horse races, in closing policy shops, faro, roulette and other gambling dens.

Put all the race courses in the United States together, then add to them all the gambling dens where poker, dice, faro, and similar games of chance are played for money, the sum total of losses and demoralization they inflicted would scarcely equal those entailed by margin gambling in railway and mining stocks, in oil, grain, provisions and cotton, in the exchanges and bucket shops at New York, Boston, Philadelphia, Baltimore, Oil City, New Orleans, San Francisco, St. Louis and Chicago.

Lame ducks and wrecks of this speculative gambling are thickly scattered here and there all over New York and the neighboring cities. They are to be found in every State and in almost every county and town that has been opened up to settlement.

Why, then, do not moralists and friends of humanity exert themselves to enlist right-minded people to agitate the matter, and to demand the enactment of laws to crush out this monstrous evil of margin gambling, short selling, and stock washing? .

State laws would not avail, for the Exchanges could step over the line from one State into another, and "go on with the dance."

What is wanted is the strong arm of National law, enforced all over the Union, to estop margin gambling. And thumb-screw, star-chamber, inquisition State laws to take the high priests of the great god Mammon by the throat and make them pay their just share of the taxable burdens of the people.

This is the true antidote against the spread of socialism, communism and anarchy, which is even now approaching the bloody horrors of a revolution.

The " Knights of Labor," as a body, are neither socialists, communists or anarchists, but, all the same, the inevitable progress of events is in that direction, and the reasons are obvious.

In France, under a profligate monarchy, the higher classes had many privileges which were denied to other subjects, especially their exemption from taxes. Common people were despised and yet made to bear all the burdens and expenses of the State.

Louis XVI., wishing to rectify this condition of affairs, and restore the disordered state of the finances, convoked the Notables, a body selected from the higher orders. To them it was proposed to lay a land tax, proportioned to property, without any exemption. This the Notables refused to sanction.

These things and other causes gave rise to the Jacobins, and culminated in a revolutionary tribunal under Marat and Robespierre.

In the " Reign of Terror " which followed, the king, the queen, and many of the nobility were brought to death by the guillotine, and the blood of thousands on thousands of victims flowed in every part of France.

Formerly the rich and powerful kept the poor in subjection by means of the military arm. A large portion of the people of Russia were serfs— slaves of the nobles. Even at home, until the late civil war, there were millions of people in slavery.

The uneducated were at the mercy of men of superior ability, and in this way the few have been able to control the many.

The march of events within recent years has

been rapid towards the material improvement and elevation of the laboring classes.

Money, everywhere, has a tendency to concentrate itself in a few hands. Capitalists form corporations to work coal and iron mines, to build factories, railroads, steamships, telegraph lines, etc. They operate to secure the largest amount of profit at the least possible cost. They exact the largest number of hours of work for the least amount of wages.

Education and a free press has taught laborers their rights, and that they can enforce their rights by combining together in societies. Hence they have their local district assemblies all over the Union and a National Assembly presided over by a General Master Workman.

Poor people generally pay no direct tax; indirectly they pay a grinding tax in increased rents, and in the enhanced cost of all the necessaries of life.

Of all combinations of capital, speculative monopoly in Wall Street is the worst. Untold millions of dollars are filched from the people year after year, by trickery and artifice, to the enrichment of private individuals. Hundreds of millions in railway bonds and other taxable personal property is kept covered up and concealed from assessment. The burden of taxation is thrown on real estate, and the landlords in turn throw it on the shoulders of their tenants in increased rents.

CHAPTER IV.

COLLAPSE OF A BULL MARKET.

FROM 1880 to 1882 the stock market had had a big rise. Speculation ran riot.

The outside public were in and biting at the bait eagerly.

Prices fluctuated up on purchases, down on realizations like the billows of the ocean, now down in the trough of the sea, now up on the crest of the waves.

The outside adventurer and alert trader could catch on and snatch frequent profits that turned his head, and lead to reckless infatuation.

Then came the collapse and the savage raids of the bears to destroy values. The insiders had sold out and gone heavily short. The outside public were stranded with stocks mostly bought on margins. They were left to get out as best they could, or to follow their banker's advice to " hold on." Those who held on on weak margins were wiped out. Many who had paid for their stocks outright were so fearfully roasted, that in the end they threw over their holdings, in terror, at enormous losses. The following table shows the highest and lowest prices of the leading active stocks for the years 1881–2, and 1883–4:

	1881. High	1881. Low	1882. High	1882. Low	1883. High	1883. Low	1884. High	1884. Low
Canada Southern	90	50	73	44	71¾	47¼	57⅞	24¾
Jersey Central	112	82½	97½	63¼	90	68¼	90	37½
Central Pacific	102⅞	80½	97⅞	86	88	61	67¾	30
St. Paul	129¼	101½	128¼	98¾	108½	91¾	94½	58¼
" Preferred	138¼	116¾	144¼	114½	122¼	115	119	98⅞
Northwestern	136	117	150¾	124	140⅛	115½	124	82¾
" Preferred	147½	131⅛	175	136	153¾	134	149½	117
Lackawanna	129	107	150¼	116½	131½	113¾	133⅛	90½
Burlington and Quincy	182½	136¾	141	120½	129⅜	117	127¾	107
Denver and Rio Grande	113¼	66	74⅝	38¼	51½	21¼	25⅝	6⅜
Bloomington and Western	100½	38⅛	49½	30	35½	17½	20¼	9
Lake Shore	135¾	118	117⅜	98	114⅛	97½	104¾	59½
Louisville and Nashville	110½	79	100¾	46½	58½	40⅝	51⅝	22½
Missouri, Kansas and Texas	54	34⅞	42½	26⅜	34⅞	19½	23¼	9½
Central Hudson	155	135⅜	138	125	129⅛	112⅜	118½	83½
Northern Pacific	51	32¾	54⅜	28¾	53⅛	23⅛	27	14
" Preferred	86½	64⅛	100⅜	66¾	90⅝	49⅜	57⅝	37¼
Oregon Trans-Continental	83	64	98¾	60	89	29⅛	34⅝	6¼
Texas and Pacific	73⅝	41½	51⅝	34	43	17⅛	22⅜	5½
Union Pacific	130⅜	107½	119¾	99⅞	104¾	86⅛	84⅝	28

A CONSCIENTIOUS BROKER.

This particular broker was a gentleman and a very honorable man, considering his business. He was not mercenary like his partner, the banker.

The banker was ravenous for commissions. To him everything was good for somebody else to buy or sell, if it brought grist to him. But he took no risks to buy or sell for himself. Not he!

Often, often this broker held his customers out of ventures that his banker partner advised them into. Many losses were thus averted at the expense of loss of commissions to the stock house.

The broker, while not advising purchases at any and all times, was a bull on principle. He never liked the bear side of the market. But it was his business to execute orders whether for the long or short account, and he did it.

The market had had a long run of prosperity. He had great faith in the soundness and stability of values of the Granger and Pacific stocks, especially in the " Villards." Many of the sharpest and shrewdest business men in New York pinned their faith to them and backed it up with their money.

When the bears began their raids on the Pacific stocks, and exposed the existing rottenness in these corporations, these men could not and would not believe it.

They held on through a decline of twenty, thirty, forty, or more per cent., and then their faith turned to distrust, doubt to conviction, and they threw over their stocks at losses of tens, hundreds of thousands and millions of dollars.

At the end of the great decline and depression these victims of misplaced confidence numbered hundreds of thousands.

The failure, or suspension of banks here and there all over the country exposed bank Presidents and Cashiers who had speculated with, and lost the money of their depositors.

Defaults brought speculative fiduciary agents, and managers of business enterprises to grief and public exposure.

But the great multitude of private individuals who slunk out of "the Street," crippled or utterly ruined, were never heard of outside the circle of their own family and friends.

THE BROKER WORRIED.

This same broker before mentioned was superior to his class ; was above petty trickery ; was "as straight as a parson," and really solicitous for the success of his customers.

About the time these heavy losses were accruing, in friendly gossip, he told the writer he "wished he was out of the business ; he could not sleep thinking of the misfortunes of his clientele." He had a boy just entering manhood, " he would not have him become a broker." " If he could hit the market three times out of five he would not be there acting as the agent of anybody but himself." At another time he talked of " going out of the business the next spring," the results to customers of the house had been so disastrous. Not unfrequently he would dissuade customers from ventures, and if the orders were insisted on, he would execute them with fear as to the result.

Some of his customers were bears on general principles; if they got caught in a corner and had to pay a loaning rate of say $400 for one day's loan of 100 shares of stock, he would denounce the manipulators of the squeeze as " thieves and robbers."

He is a broker still, and on being asked why he did not go out of business as he expected to, he replied : " I cannot help it, I have no other occupation."

CHAPTER V.

MANIPULATING BANKER-BROKERS.

GENERALLY they are men with large capital. On occasion they can form a "combine" with other capitalists and millionaires, and make up a pool of fifty or a hundred million dollars to boom the market.

Such combinations are all powerful. They can advance prices at their will. Sometimes they confine themselves to certain specialties, at other times they include almost the whole speculative list.

To begin, they talk down prices and encourage outside short selling. All this time they are quietly picking up block after block of good dividend-paying stocks, as a basis for a future movement.

When prices are low and the market is dull they can take weeks or months to get things in train for an advance.

All being ready, the news agencies are made a factor to circulate news and rumors of bull pools and a boom in prices. The buying through various stock houses is more open and decided, prices begin to mount up fraction by fraction, point by point.

The bears run to cover and their purchases help
on the advance.   At ten points, or so, up, prices
may be allowed to sag down under realizations.·
Things may remain in this position one or more
weeks to encourage the bears to put out fresh
lines of shorts.

The pools loan their stocks freely.   The bears
have no trouble in borrowing from day to day to
keep good their deliveries.

A good short interest having been roped in,
another advance is started, and the bears again
take to cover.   This may put prices up 15 or 20
per cent.

The insiders begin to trade on their holdings.   They sell hundreds or thousands of shares
at the top, and let prices run off from two to
five points.   Then they buy back their stocks
at the bottom.   They repeat these manœuvers
from time to time.   Then, perhaps, rumors will
be circulated that times are not favorable for
a further advance, or that the " big men " are
unloading.   Every inducement is thrown out to
encourage the bears to sell short.   Stocks are
plenty in the " loan crowd," and can be had for
the asking.

A PIRATICAL METHOD.

A short interest of from one to three, or four
hundred thousand shares having accumulated,
loaned stock is suddenly called in.   In one or

more specialties the bears can borrow no stock to keep good their deliveries, except at a premium. There is a corner. The loaning rate for a day or two may be one-eighth or $12.50 on each 100 shares. The price of the stock is run up.

Timid bears rush to cover at a loss. Stubborn ones hold out in hopes the "squeeze" will pass over. The advance in one or more stocks strengthens the whole market, and the entire list goes up in sympathy.

In the height of the squeeze the loaning rate is suddenly run up to, perhaps, $400 per day on each 100 shares. This is too much for the most obstinate bruin. There is a bear panic and they rush pell-mell to cover. Prices advance five or ten points under their purchases in buying in the stocks they sold, but did not have to sell.

The bulls are now unloading at enormous profits, and getting a big loaning rate besides. The bear who buys stock "regular" cannot get his stock until the next day. In the meantime he must borrow to keep good his delivery. The stock he borrows one day may be wanted the next, and he must return it and get a loan somewhere else.

He can close out his deal and avoid the high loaning rate for that day, by buying "cash" stock for immediate delivery to him. With this he makes his final delivery and is free. The difference in price between "cash" and that bought "regular," is sometimes from five to six per cent.

All these transactions of borrowing and returning stock are fixed through the broker in the board room.

ANOTHER PIRATICAL METHOD.

In 1882 Oregon Trans-Continental stock reached its highest apex, 98¾. Up to July, 1883, it ranged up and down between that price and 75½. In the great bear raids which set in during the latter part of 1883, and continued into 1884, the fall in the price of the "Villard stocks," viz., Oregon Trans-Continental, Northern Pacific, common and preferred, and Oregon Railway and Navigation, was fearful.

One afternoon " O. T." closed at about 45, and opened next morning at the same figure. The bears had organized their forces, and a vigorous raid set in against it. It went down by fractions, quarters, halves and whole points between quotations.

Frightened holders ordered their brokers to sell them out at market. Down, down went the price until it reached 30. Ten and fifteen per cent. margins were wiped out like magic.

When suddenly, as if by the interposition of swift-winged Mercury, the raid was stayed. The bulls flew to the rescue. Buying orders came into the Board fast and furious. The bears wavered, turned to cover, almost jumped over each other, yelling like demons their bids to recover the stocks they had sold while there was yet a profit.

Up, up went the price as fast as it had gone down, until the buying fever exhausted itself at 41. The stock had a fall of $15 a share, and a recovery of $11, all within the short space of half an hour.

CHAPTER VI.

SURE POINTS—METHOD OF A ROTHSCHILD—THE
PYRAMIDS—JENA—AUSTERLITZ—MARENGO.

NAPOLEON I., by the prestige of military success became the terror of Europe. Kings and potentates trembled at the magic of his name. Financial interests were fearfully depressed.

The disastrous Russian campaign, the retreat from Moscow, his troops impeded in their flight by deep snows, decimated by intense cold and the fierce attacks on flank and rear by the hardy Cossacks of the Don and the Volga, left him but the remnant of a demoralized army, and eventually caused his ruin.

Money values revived for a time, until Napoleon raised a fresh army of 350,000 men and hazarded all on the great battle of Leipsic, where he was crushed in the collision with the Russians, Prussians and Austrians.

The entry of the allied armies into Paris caused the temporary collapse of the French empire and consigned him to exile on the island of Elba.

Then for a time confidence was restored. All Europe became tranquil. Stocks and government funds rallied with buoyancy.

Suddenly Napoleon reappeared, resumed the reins of empire, gathered together his veteran troops, and filled their depleted ranks by conscriptions from every nook and corner of France.

All was excitement and apprehension. Stocks and consols were again in the doldrums in London and on all the bourses of the Continent.

It was a critical time for England when Nathan Meyer Rothschild, then head of the great London house of his name, secretly crossed over into Belgium, and, on horseback, from the top of a hill, with a powerful field-glass, watched the momentous events transpiring on the plain of Waterloo.

Reconnoitering just long enough to see the national colors of France trailing in the dust and to make sure that the lucky star of Napoleon had set, he put spurs to his horse, rode with all speed to the nearest seaport, hired the fastest vessel he could get to put him across the North Sea. On the morning of his arrival in London he appeared in his usual place by the " Rothschild pillar," in the temple of Mammon.

Did he spread the glorious tidings which would have set all England in ecstasy: the triumph of the Royal Standard of St. George over the Imperial Eagles of France? Not he !

Gloom hung like a pall over every household from the palace of the King to the hut of the peasant. All awaited with bated breath for news of fateful import.

Crafty as Machiavel, cunning as Tallyrand, Rothschild, inwardly chuckling, outwardly assuming a serious mien and gloomy tone, talked dubiously of the fortunes of war, while covertly he spurred on his confidential agents to buy up all the stocks and consols they could lay their hands upon.

His information was a day in advance of the arrival of couriers from the Duke of Wellington, and when they did arrive with the news of the downfall of Napoleon there was a tremendous rebound, not only in public feeling, but in the value of securities, out of which this thrifty knight of the " Red Shield " reaped a harvest of millions of pounds sterling, almost in a trice.

A BOURBON METHOD.

Nowhere were the uncertainties, always following upon finance, greater than under the surprises and excitements attending and intervening between the first and second French empires.

The empire was succeeded by a kingdom, that by a revolution, which gave way to a new king. Then came a quasi-republic, to be succeeded by the coup d'etat of Napoleon III.

Among so mercurial a people the health of the sovereign had a most potent influence on speculation. The bare anticipation of a change of rulers gave rise to fears of internal revolution between the legitimists, the Bonapartists and the republicans, and was a powerful factor in depressing the stock market.

Kings and princes are as great gamblers as any other class. King Louis Philippe was as adroit and crafty in the acquisition of money as any financier of his time. He speculated secretly with immense success. When prices were high he sold out his stocks and rentes, and went heavily short of the market. Then he would feign illness and take to his bed.

No doubt the physicians of his court were particeps criminis in the deception. Daily and hourly bulletins would be sent out. The King was growing from bad to worse, from dangerous to critical.

Down, down went the price of stocks and rentes. At the proper time his agents, at his order, quietly covered his shorts and bought up large lines of securities for the long account.

The trick having been consummated the King would recover by easy stages. The profits on both sides of the deal would be princely.

When he next appeared before the populace he would be greeted with shouts of "Vive le roi." But what would his subjects have thought had they known he had been through their pockets like a pirate?

CHAPTER VII.

PRESENT METHODS.

IN these days of electric telegraphs, telephones and railway trains news travels fast. Still the insiders in the market get sure points of more or less value in ample time to discount their information before the outsiders are allowed half a chance. On fluctuations of from one to five points, the ins have played the winning cards before the outs can get the news and act on it ; and if they do act on it, they are generally made the dupes of the insiders, who are then ready to realize profits at their expense.

Often half a dozen capitalists may be directors of as many different railroad, steamship and telegraph companies. They have advance information of matters affecting their corporations, whether the earnings are increasing or decreasing, if dividends are to be reduced or passed, or defaults are to occur in the payment of interest on bonds.

There are always a more or less number of speculative capitalists in the National Legislature. During the sessions of Congress, bills, affecting steamship subsidies, the extension of indebtedness of railroads to the Government, the confirmation or forfeiture of railway land grants, etc., are allowed to drag along for months or from one session to another.

Cipher dispatches pass between the Washington ring of speculators, in and out of office, and their copartners in New York. Leading operators go to the Capitol on stock-jobbing missions.

Presently the news appears that this bill or that bill will be called up in committee, or before the Senate or House, on a certain date, and favorable or unfavorable action had upon it. Too often this is a ruse to affect the stock market. The public are led in long or short. Stocks go up or go down on the expected action to be had on bills.

The bill comes up in due time, and after some jugglery is laid on the table, only to be called up again and again at future times for stock-jobbing purposes, before final action is had and the bill disposed of.

Those who buy or sell for short turns generally find the effect is discounted in advance.

Points and tips are manufactured to order by financial writers. Sometimes they are straight, but more often very crooked steers for the public to be guided by.

PANIC IN PACIFIC MAIL.

The Pacific Mail Steamship Company had a subsidy of $95,000 per month for carrying heavy freight around to California via the Isthmus, for the Union and Central Pacific Railroads. It also had a large subsidy from the Government for carrying the U. S. Mail.

In the Spring of 1885 the stock had been boomed up to 63, then the price fell back to about 58, and people were tempted to buy it. To the writer's knowledge one man, connected with large shipping interests, bought 500 shares of it just before the close of business one afternoon.

The next morning the news was in all the city papers that the Union Pacific Company had given notice to the P. M. S. S. Co. of the withdrawal of the subsidy in one month's time. This was followed by a notice from the Central Pacific to the same effect.

At the opening of business that morning the news was all over "the Street," and there was a panic to get out of it. Bulls threw it over and bears pitched in and sold it heavily short. It was said that fully three-fourths of the stock of the par value of $20,000,000 was thrown over, besides what the bears sold. Prices tumbled in about two days to 46¾.

Subsequently it was openly charged and never disputed that certain directors in Pacific Mail and in Union and Central Pacific had advance information of what was coming in time to enable them to sell out their stock and go heavily short of it. This accounted for the previous drop from 63 to 58.

The springing of such a mine on a confiding public only illustrates the heartless character of Wall Street speculation.

Afterwards the loss of its steamer, the "City of Tokio," valued at $1,250,000, near Yokohama, Japan, and the loss of the Government mail subsidy, by the action of Postmaster-General Vilas, added to the Company's troubles.   •

The man who bought the 500 shares mentioned held on to his stock and eventually came out with a good profit. In the summer of 1885 the payment of a subsidy by the Pacific railroads was resumed, and in the fall the stock was boomed up to 70.

In the spring of 1886, on the breaking out of the Trans-Continental troubles, the Pacific railroads again broke the freight subsidy, and up to March, 1887, it has not been resumed. It also suffered the loss of another steamer, the " Honduras," on the Pacific coast, valued at $250,000. The Company was said to insure its own steamers, and, if so, the loss was total.

The Company paid five per cent. dividends on its stock from 1884 to January, 1886; since which time the dividends have been passed.

Taking a long course of years as a criterion, Pacific Mail stock has been the most erratic and has had the widest fluctuations, in price. of any other stock on the speculative list.

From 1865, down to the present time, its price

has been anywhere between $329 and $10.37½ a share. Just think of it ; $32,900 for 100 shares, at one time, and only $1,037.50 for the same stuff at another time.

A SPECULATIVE METHOD.

Not so very long ago the President of a certain railroad company was quoted as saying very positively "that certain speculative capitalists had proposed to him to let the management of the road run down in order to apparently depreciate the property and thus force creditors to sell their claims at much less than their real value!"

This brought forth the following newspaper comment : "A more rascally suggestion never came from persons admitted to the society of honorable men. It was nothing less than a proposal to rob honest creditors under cover of a plot involving treachery and false pretences. And yet these men, by reason of the position and influence which their wealth gives them, are able to go their way as if nothing had happened to lower them in the good opinion of the world."

This matter was afterwards inquired into and whitewashed by a committee of the State Legislature.

CALIFORNIA SPECULATIONS.

STORY OF THE RISE AND FALL OF A SAN FRAN-
CISCO BOOK-KEEPER.

[*San Francisco Letter in Sacramento Bee.*]

I am confident that the romance of stock-gambling will never be written. Life here is too rapid, too pushing for men to pause and reflect on that curious "has been" of San Francisco. But I never stroll down Pine Street, or linger in the shadows of Pauper Alley, but I meet some one who would be entitled to a place in that unwritten romance. The tall figure, a face clean-cut and refined, gait slow and painful from the effect of an old wound, is before me as I write. James D. Walker, ten years ago, was a member of the bonanza firm, and his check was good for $500,000, aye, a million, at any bank in the country. Then Flood and Fair bought him out, and Walker opened a broker's office under the Nevada Bank, and did all the business of his former partners. In these times Flood, Fair and Mackay were on the top notch of speculation. They were swinging the market at their own sweet will, and making or breaking the thousands who were battling with the fierce tide of stock-gambling. Alexander Austin, or "Sandy," as his friends used to call him, had just served his term as tax collector, and went in with Walker. How they did make things boom! The

high-salaried clerks—the book-keeper got $400 a
month and had a sumptuous lunch served every
day in a large room at the rear of the office at
the expense of the firm. Their expenses were
enormous, but so was their business. The partners
were clearing $20,000 a month, but they were
standing on the brink of a precipice. Flood re-
marked that other and outside speculators were
manipulating certain stock precisely as his own
brokers. This would never do, so he called a consultation, and informed the Walker firm that this
sort of thing would not do ; that there was a traitor in the camp somewhere, and that unless he
was detected and fired their relations could not
continue. Close and earnest investigation was
made, but without avail. Then came a transaction of more than ordinary importance, but to the
intense disgust of the bonanza firm it was apparently foreseen and anticipated by these same outside brokers, who were kept posted, apparently,
by some traitor in the Walker-Austin camp.
Then the bonanza people changed their broker,
and from that hour the fortunes of Walker & Co.
began to decline. Matters grew worse and worse.
Austin committed suicide. Walker sold a magnificent mansion in Oakland, which cost him close
on $500,000, to prop up the waning glory of the
swell firm. At last it was a clean case of bust,
and I don't believe Mr. Walker to-day could put
his hand on $200. I saw him looking wistfully at

the Nevada Bank building, probably comparing the different states of Flood, the member, and Walker, the ex-member of the bonanza firm. He discovered, when too late, that the high-priced book-keeper was the traitor. He sold his employers, but no luck ever came of his treachery, and he is to-day keeping books at $50 a month for a Hebrew clothes dealer in Portland, Oregon.

Walker is but a type of hundreds of others who have had their chance and their day on Pine Street. With a strange fatuity these wrecks still cling to the locality where they made and lost fortunes in the past, though nine-tenths of them have not a dime to speculate with and could not get credit for a glass of lager, when their names a decade ago were sufficient guarantee for a dozen or fifty dozen cases of champagne. A few have pulled out with a small stake, and there are some there on the Street yet who have a little money and would speculate if they saw an opening, and not a few fanatics who await the coming of the Messiah —the discovery of another great bonanza.

CHAPTER VIII.

NORTHERN PACIFIC RAILROAD.

FROM its inception in 1864 to the driving of the "golden spike" on the completion of the main line in 1883, the construction of the Northern Pacific Railway was attended by a series of misfortunes to all who meddled with it, almost unparalleled in the history of railroad building. In the magnitude of losses inflicted on innocent and confiding people, the "Credit Mobilier" was completely overshadowed by it.

In the beginning the most enticing advertisements were kept inserted in the leading secular and religious newspapers, setting forth the safety and certainty of the payment of interest on its bonds, which were offered to investors at about 92, and accrued interest at 7–30 per cent.

The small savings of clergymen, widows, the estates of orphans and others were drawn into it. Large numbers of people who had money to spare were cajoled into the investment.

Interest on the bonds first issued was paid from the proceeds of other bonds when sold, and from sales of stock.

In 1875 the Company defaulted in the payment

of interest and the road was sold under foreclosure. The proceeds of the sale were not sufficient to satisfy the bonds and past due interest,
hence the stock was wiped out.

A committee of bondholders bought in the road,
and $1,400 par value of new preferred stock was
issued for each $1,000 bond and past due interest.
Those who depended on the interest of their
investments to pay necessary living expenses now
had to take stock which from that time to this has
paid them no income whatever.

In 1883 a scrip dividend of $11\frac{1}{10}$ per cent.
was paid on the preferred stock, but this was not
cash. It was equivalent to the issue of so much
new stock which bore no cumulative income.

Jay Cooke, a very rich man, became President
of the Company and chief promoter in building
the road, was himself overwhelmed in the disaster
attending the enterprise.

After the foreclosure, the Company was reorganized, and the building of the road was continued with money obtained by the issue of new
bonds, stock and proceeds from land sales.

The road had an enormous land grant from the
Government, equivalent to 12,800 acres per mile
in the States and 25,600 acres per mile in the
Territories.

Its stock capitalization now is nearly $40,000,000
of preferred and $49,000,000 of common stock.
Its preferred stock (at present writing worth about

60) is received at par in payment for its lands east of the Mississippi River, and the stock canceled.

The senseless, crazy character of the bull speculation in 1881–2 cannot be better illustrated than in the Oregon Trans-Continental mania which carried away millions of investors' money.

The basis of the venture was the Oregon Railway and Navigation Company, which had no competition, and earned handsome dividends transporting the products of the rich State of Oregon.

Money was wanted to push the Northern Pacific Railway to completion. Henry Villard became President of the corporation, and to obtain money conceived the idea of a Construction Còmpany. So the Oregon Trans-Continental Co. was brought into life with a capital stock of $50,000,000, of which $40,000,000 was issued, and was eagerly grabbed for.

Villard got all the money he needed from the proceeds of the sale of O. T. stock, and bought up Oregon Railway and Navigation, Northern Pacific common and preferred stocks, until the control of those companies was secured and transferred to the O. T. Co., with Villard as President of them all.

The O. R. and N. stock paid dividends of 10 per cent. N. P. preferred paid a scrip dividend of $11\frac{1}{10}$ per cent., and in January, 1883, O. T. began to pay dividends of 6 per cent. in cash.

All these stocks were enormously inflated in

1882. The highest prices were: O. R. and N.,
163¼; N. P. preferred, 103⅜; N. P. common, 54⅝;
and O. T., 95¼.

The issue of O. T. stock was a master stroke.
Villard was a star on the financial horizon. The
manipulation of his stocks on the market was
adroit and successful, and the N. P. Railway was
brought to completion.

But it was at a fearful expense, not only to a
confiding public, but to the insiders in it. Villard
himself was caught in the whirlwind, and the bulk
of his fortune was swept away like a dream.

It was easy to hold up quotations and advance
them as long as money could be had for the asking. But every purse has its bottom, and even
Villard's was reached, when the public were obliged
to sell on the discovery that O. T. was getting
entirely dependent on O. R. and N. 10 per cent.
dividends. And that any dividends on N. P. preferred were impossible, because its reported earnings were for transportation of construction material for its own road.

The purchasing power of Oregon Trans-Continental was exhausted. Confidence was gone. The
end of its tether was reached. The bubble had
burst, there were no earnings for dividends and
no public to buy surplusage of stock.

The bears had nosed out all the weak points in
the armor of these corporations. They made capital out of the fact that a great part of the road

was built through a wilderness, and built ten to fifteen years in advance of the settlement and growth of a profitable freight business along its line.

The Northern Pacific was built eastward from Puget Sound and Portland, Oregon, and westward from Superior City, Wisconsin. The two ends of the road met, the last rail was laid, and Mr. Vil_ lard, accompanied by a junketing party of American and foregn capitalists, went out to celebrate the event on September 8, 1883, by the driving of the last—a golden spike.

It was more like driving a nail into his own coffin, for the bear organs were filling the whole speculative atmosphere with blue ruin and disaster to these specialties.

In the fore part of September, 1883, insiders were getting out. There was no other outlook except severe and continued liquidation, which set in the last half of September with such energy it could not be checked until it had run its course.

Confidence was undermined, values crumbled away, until at the end of the year 1883 O. R. and N. stock had declined to 90 ; N. P. preferred to $49\frac{3}{8}$; N. P. common to $23\frac{5}{8}$, and O. T. to $29\frac{1}{8}$. Liquidation in these stocks continued in 1884 and the lowest prices reached were O. R. and N., $60\frac{3}{4}$; N. P. preferred, $37\frac{1}{4}$; N. P. common, 14, and O. T., $6\frac{1}{4}$.

Dividends on O. R. and N. were reduced to 6

per cent., those on O. T. were passed. The O. T. as a construction company had accomplished its mission. Now the O. T. stock is intrinsically worth pro rata in the ratio of the market value of its holdings of Oregon Navigation and the Northern Pacific stocks.

Mr. Villard resigned the Presidencies of the Companies one after the other and retired to Europe, for a time, a thoroughly demoralized man. In the height of his prosperity he was reputed worth $5,000,000, out of which it was estimated he saved half a million from the crash. Such was the origin and the end of the famous "blind pool."

Although built in advance of the influx of population, it is very rich in future possibilties. Prudently managed and not too closely paralleled by other roads, the Northern Pacific is destined to become, in time, one of the most magnificent railway properties in the western world.

LUCK IN WALL STREET.

A FORTUNE OF $2,000,000 ROLLED UP IN FOUR YEARS.

Broker and Sunday-school Superintendent —— —— —— - is understood to have made about $200,000 in Wall Street during the last month, and he is now worth, it is estimated, $2,000,000. He is a member of the firm of —— —— ——

and is the Superintendent of a Methodist Sunday school.

His luck in the market has been phenomenal, and his moves have been so bold and successful that he has been as much a central figure as ——— ——— ———. His fortune has all been made in four years. At the beginning of the decline in 1880, he was worth, perhaps, $100,000. He then sold Wabash at the top figures—around 96½— and did not cover until 56 was touched. On the reaction he went short again and followed the stock down to about 35. Few men have made money faster than he did in that deal. He was short before the May panic last year. He covered up his stocks at a profit a few days previous to the crash, and went to Philadelphia to attend a religious convention. While he was away the panic took place. Had he kept out his shorts, which he would have done if he had remained in town, he would have made an additional profit of $250,000 in the smash.

The lowest prices were touched the last of June, 1884. He started to bull the market immediately afterwards, and picked out the stocks that afterwards showed profits. He was loaded up with stocks in the last rise and made great gains in St. Paul, Lackawanna, Northwest, Union Pacific, Western Union and Lake Shore.

He never was an ardent admirer of Mr. Gould, and has had little to do with that speculator. He was on the side of S. H. Kneeland and against Gould in the elevated railway fight up to the time of the settlement and consolidation of the roads. Gould has on many occasions recognized his strength in the market and invited him to confer with him.

Mr. ———— yells with all the lustiness of a cowboy in the Stock Exchange. He is a man of excellent taste in dress, although his clothes are of a quiet nature. He deals in figures of speech in conversation that are always to the point and are likewise very taking. He has dark hair, which he parts on the side, and a dark mustache. When talking he usually picks up a piece of paper, which he abstractedly pulls to pieces or twirls. He is a patron of art, and at his residence in Madison avenue has a collection of pictures worth $100,000. As he is a good judge his works include few poor examples.—*N. Y. World*, 1886.

CHÀPTER IX.

UNION AND CENTRAL PACIFIC RAILWAYS.

DURING the administration of Franklin Pierce Congress ordered several surveys to be made to ascertain the feasibility of connecting California and the East by railroads.

In 1863 Government aid was extended, the companies incorporated, and the work of construction was begun.

The Central Pacific was built eastward from San Francisco to Ogden, Utah, a distance of 883 miles of main line. A land grant of millions of acres was given by Act of Congress, also large subsidies in United States bonds, for which the Government took long-term liens.

The Union Pacific was built westward from Omaha, Nebraska, connecting with the Central Pacific at Ogden. The through line from Omaha to San Francisco, a distance of 1,900 miles, was completed in 1869.

The Union Pacific had a land grant of 12,800 acres per mile, and a United States Bond subsidy of upwards of $27,000,000, also on long-term liens. On the extension of its road and branch lines it secured a large additional subsidy and several more millions of acres of the public lands.

This Company was formed by a consolidation of the Union Pacific, the Kansas Pacific and the Denver Pacific. Altogether it had a United States Bond subsidy of over $33,500,000, and a land grant estimated at 18,083,227 acres.

The Union Pacific and Central Pacific were not making their payments on the Government liens as required by the Act of 1864. By the " Thurman " Act of 1878, one-half the charges for Government transportation were to be withheld, and the Central Pacific was to pay $1,200,000 per annum into a sinking fund towards the extinction of its debt. Similar obligations were also imposed on the U. P., but neither Company has lived up to them.

In the recent exposures by the New York *World*, the united debts of these two companies to the Government, for principal and interest, is stated at the enormous sum of over $157,000,000.

The " Pacific Railroad Ring " has long maintained a powerful and ravenous lobby at Washington. Its objective point is to secure the passage of a " seventy or eighty year extension bill " at a nominal interest of about three per cent. on their debts.

The *World* fights the " extension bill " tooth and nail, and says : " The result, even if the payments were made in good faith, would be the pay-

6

ment by the companies of eleven-twelfths of the interest due, and a virtual gift to these corporations of about $150,000,000 of the principal."

The stock, bonded and other debts of the U. P. are estimated at over $200,000,000, and those of the C. P. at over $160,000,000.

Had these roads been managed with prudence and economy in the interest of their stockholders, they would now be in a highly prosperous condition. Their obligations to the Government, all fixed charges and debts as they became due, might have been promptly met and good dividends paid on the stock.

Instead of this, the Union Pacific, almost from first to last, has been the El Dorado of all the arch conspirators in the country, in and out of Congress. Its stock has been alternately inflated and depressed to the enrichment of railroad wreckers, at the expense of a deluded public.

The U. P. paid dividends of from $5\frac{1}{2}$ to $6\frac{3}{4}$ per cent. from 1878 to 1881, then 7 per cent. to 1884, when dividends were passed.

The C. P. paid 6 per cent. from 1880 to 1884, when the dividends stopped.

The highest price of U. P. was $130\frac{5}{8}$ in 1881, and the lowest, $28 per share in 1884. C. P.'s highest and lowest was $102\frac{1}{4}$ and $30 per share.

There is one peculiarity about Central Pacific stock which makes many operators shy clear of it at any price. That is the personal liability attached to it. By the laws of California, if the Company fails to meet its obligations to that State and its citizens, the stock can be assessed for the deficit on all who hold it.

Some bankers even hate to carry it for customers, in their own name, and instances can be cited in which they have carried the stock in the name of irresponsible clerks.

In 1882-3 sharp business men, of large and small capital, were fooled and deceived by the atmosphere of over-confidence in the value and stability of railway securities. They would not believe the arguments of the bears until the financial storm had burst with all its fury, and involved them in immense losses.

Union Pacific had strong friends. Millionaire investors and others believed in it. Some had stock bought at 110 and upwards. They held on to it and bought more in the 90s, 80s and 70s to average up. Some accumulated ten, twenty, thirty thousand shares before they called a halt.

All this time the bears were working their batteries of denunciation of the utter worthlessness of the stock. It was openly talked in "the Street" that it was not worth $5 a share intrinsically.

Down, down went the price, and the passing of the dividend in 1884 added to the pressure to sell. In the 50s, 40s and 30s holders were throwing it over, in some cases at losses of hundreds of thousands of dollars.

The stock had been paying dividends, while defaulting in the payment of its obligations to the Government, and the actual condition of affairs was kept covered up and concealed by a peculiar system of book-keeping.

U. P. went to 28, and would have gone lower had not Jay Gould asserted his power to stay the decline by purchasing large blocks of it. Doubtless he made a profitable turn when the price was sent spinning up to 58 three months after.

Central Pacific went to 30 and would probably have declined in as great a ratio as U. P., but for the strong hold Stanford, Crocker and Huntington had on it.

When Charles Francis Adams, Jr., assumed the Presidency of Union Pacific in place of Sidney Dillon, a radical change in the management was inaugurated, which the friends of the Company hoped would extricate it from its difficulties. But until their obligations to the Government are in some way adjusted, it is not probable that either of these roads can resume the payment of dividends.

CHAPTER X.

EVENTS PRECEDING PANIC OF 1884.

FOR five years previous to 1883 the building of new railroads was unprecedented. Many thousand miles were built ; some into new thinly settled regions in the West and Southwest.

Others paralleled old roads which had ample facilities for all the business contiguous to their lines for years to come.

The Lake Shore was paralleled for about 500 miles by the N. Y., Chicago and St. Louis ("Nickel Plate"). The N. Y., West Shore and Buffalo was being constructed almost alongside the great four-track N. Y. C. H. R. R. for about 450 miles.

In the boom from 1878 to 1882 the public became loaded up with a mass of stocks and bonds of new companies, and other securities, issued on consolidations of old companies.

All this stuff was floated in the general activity. Those who bought it afterwards found there was no prospect of dividends on stocks, or interest on many classes of bonds, for years to come.

With no income and the value of their securities depreciating, the public began to liquidate in

1883. In the fall of that year came the great break in the "Villard" stocks, following the driving of the "golden spike," completing the main line of the Northern Pacific Railway.

January, 1884, found the speculative public depressed and demoralized. A large short interest was outstanding, and in the latter part of the month combinations were formed to drive the bears to cover. This advanced prices and kept things steady until March.

Strong bull pools bought up large lines of Del., Lack. and Western and N. Y. Central, and in March there was a corner in "Lack.," which carried the price up from 123 to $133\frac{1}{8}$ regular, and $139\frac{1}{2}$ for cash stock. Shorts in N. Y. C. were also squeezed, and the price run up from $113\frac{1}{4}$ to 122.

All the other market strengthened up in sympathy and demoralized the bears for a time. But large holders took advantage of the strength to feed out the stocks they had been carrying. This caused a fluctuating and gradually declining market until May.

THE PANIC.

The rascalities of Ferdinand Ward culminated in the suspension of the Marine Bank on May 6th, and the house of Grant & Ward was reported in trouble for about half a million dollars.

On May 9th Grant & Ward were reported irretrievably ruined, and Ward's residence in Brook-

lyn was seized by the Sheriff and placed in charge
of a deputy. Ward was shadowed night and day
by a dozen private detectives until arrested on
May 21st.

On May 14th the panic was begun by stock
brokers and speculators throwing their stocks on
the market, owing to the great shrinkage in values.

George I. Seney's Metropolitan Bank suspended, and its correspondent, the Atlantic Bank of
Brooklyn, followed. About half a score of brokers went under, and other failures were believed to
be impending.

On May 15th the Clearing House Banks united
together to support each other, by the issue of
Clearing House certificates. This checked the
panic somewhat, and enabled the Metropolitan
Bank to resume. Manager W. A. Camp, of the Clearing House said : " That Institution was ready to
lend the Metropolitan Bank any amount from one
million to five millions of dollars." George I.
Seney resigned as President of the bank. The
discovery was made that the Second National
Bank had been robbed of about three million dollars through the stock speculations of its President. This loss was immediately made good by
his father and other directors, and there was no
hiatus in the business of the bank.

The morning papers, the same day, had reported the failure of —— —— ——, President and
chief promoter of the Bankers' and Merchants'

Telegraph Company. On the opening of business at the Exchange this stock quickly dropped down 60 per cent. or more.

Fisk & Hatch failed, and Mr. Hatch, who was President of the Stock Exchange, resigned. The general market declined from 1 to 5 per cent.

On May 16th the panic was continued amid great excitement. The Newark, N. J., Savings Institution suspended payment. An attache of the house of Grant & Ward reported: "All we know at present is that our liabilities are between twelve and fourteen million dollars."

On May 17th the panic and excitement was continued and two more failures were reported.

On May 19th the Associated Banks and the Sub-Treasury took measures to stop the panic, and confidence began to be restored.

On May 21st Ferdinand Ward was summoned before the Grand Jury for examination. He was arrested during the day and remained all night at the Sinclair House in charge of a Deputy Sheriff.

On May 22d Ward, pale and haggard, was committed to Ludlow Street Jail.

On May 26th James D. Fish, President of the Marine Bank, was arrested and released on giving a bail bond with sureties in $30,000.

On May 27th the dishonored President of the Second National Bank skipped to join the rogues' colony in Canada.

About the time all these events were transpiring the Bank of the Manhattan Company was robbed of $150,000 by a dishonest Teller.

During all this time while the panic lasted, the general public, who had invested their money in Wall Street, demoralized by fear and distrust, were throwing over their stocks at immense losses.

The panic was precipitated by the discovery of a line of gigantic frauds hitherto unmatched in our financial history. The worst of these frauds was perpetrated through the influence of the name, but not with the knowledge and connivance of, the great Soldier-President, Gen. U. S. Grant.

From 1861, until he got into Wall Street, Gen. Grant was a Mascot, *i. e.*, the very impersonation of good luck. In war and in peace his career was one continued success, until his unfortunate connection with Ferdinand Ward.

The office of Grant & Ward was on the basement floor of the United Bank Building at Broadway and Wall Street. Gen. Grant himself was President of the Mexican Central Railway Co., and had his office on an upper floor of the same building.

He usually came through the hall, to go up in the elevator to his office, about 10 o'clock A. M., sometimes stopping in the lower office awhile to chat. Almost invariably he puffed away at a strong cigar and presented a picture of a man self-satisfied, contented and happy with himself and all the world.

No man knowingly standing on the brink of a volcano, ready to burst under his feet, could have shown such an appearance of prosperity and *sang froid* as he did up to the time of the crash.

It was one of the characteristics of Gen. Grant, that when he put implicit trust in a man, his confidence in that man could hardly be shaken by anything short of an earthquake.

He trusted Ward and believed his stories of the great profits that were being realized in the business. He was led to believe that he and his boys had millions of dollars of undivided profits in the firm.

When the full extent of Ward's rascality was revealed, in which Gen. Grant's great name was involved in a defalcation of millions of dollars, the change in him was fearful.

During the panic the bears were in their glory. They were—figuratively—growing fat off the carcasses of the bulls.

Imagine the sacking of Magdeburgh, think of cities looted, given up to slaughter, pillage and rapine ; then the reader has a good idea of the slaughter of values, the sacking and pillage of unsophisticated " lambs " who had become entangled in the vicarious business of stock speculation.

For four or five days the streets in the vicinity of the Stock Exchange might have recalled to mind the legends of the hordes of Goths and Vandals who overran the Roman Empire.

Nondescript people flocked in from all quarters. New Street was full of them. They overflowed into Exchange Place, Broadway, Wall and Broad Streets, reminding one of the late Charles Reade's story of the Lion and the Eland.

In an opening of the forest a lordly lion had pounced on an eland, and while he tore away at his prey, lion cubs, hyenas, jackals and vultures, licking their jaws, and uttering discordant, chattering cries, formed a circle around, ludicrous to behold.

A simile : The hordes of nondescript people in the streets were typical of the lion cubs, hyenas, jackals and vultures hungry for a share of the spoils. The eland was the general public being pillaged of their money, while the lion was the demon of demoralization and plunder within the "bear garden" keeping the outside rabble at bay.

CHAPTER XI.

A SUCCESSFUL OPERATOR.

NEXT to Jay Gould and the late W. H. Vanderbilt, probably the most prominent figure in speculation of late years was the late Charles F. Woerishoffer.

He, Addison Cammack and Henry N. Smith, since the death of President Garfield, were the greatest, and, excepting Smith, the most successful bears in Wall Street.

Woerishoffer's risks were terrific, at times 200,000 shares on the short side.

Just think of a combination on the bull side against him at such a time, and a sudden advance of ten per cent. above the selling price of his shorts. The loss would have figured $2,000,000.

A jump of 20 per cent. advance on him would figure $4,000,000. And if a loaning rate of $400 per day on each 100 shares was imposed, that of itself would be $800,000 for one day.

Were the stocks he was short of concentrated in a few strong hands, such results could have been brought about before he could recover his stocks, or make a private settlement.

But Woerishoffer was not the man to take such

enormous risks, unless he knew that the bulk of stocks were widely distributed, in the hands of those who could not combine.

Many years ago just such a combination was formed against Jacob Little, the Great Bear. Erie stock had been boomed above its real value. He sold it heavily short on options. All his contracts were eagerly taken by his rivals. By the time these contracts became due all the stock had been withdrawn beyond his reach for delivery. In the opinion of " the Street " he was a ruined man. It happened that Mr. Little held certificates of indebtedness against the Erie Company for which stock was to be issued in exchange. On the eventful day he went to the office of the Erie Company and demanded the stock called for by his certificates. With this stock Mr. Little settled his contracts to the discomfiture of his opponents.

Woerishoffer occasionally suffered immense losses, but more frequently made enormous profits, At the time of his death, in the Spring of 1886, his fortune was estimated as high as $10,000,000, and not below $5,000,000 in any event.

He was born at Geinhausen, in the Province of Hesse, in 1843, came to America in 1865, and entered a stock house as clerk. In 1868 he secured a seat in the Stock Exchange, founded the house of Woerishoffer & Co., and soon had a large clientele of Dutch and German bankers and speculators.

He became the most active speculator in "the Street," and employed more brokers than any other operator, except Jay Gould. He was known to have paid as high as $500,000 a year in commissions to brokers for executing his orders. His brokers were all over Wall Street. It was impossible to detect his hand in the market when he attempted concealment, for the brokers of his own house were never sure but that the man opposite and at cross purposes had precisely the same client.

The extent of his operations was colossal, sometimes as high as 50,000 shares in a single day. His following among the Germans and others was immense.

One of the things which won him repute was a fight, in 1879, with Gould, Sage and other capitalists interested in securing the control of the Kansas Pacific Railroad Company. As the representative of Frankfort investors, Woerishoffer had contracted to sell certain Denver extension bonds to the Gould-Sage syndicate at 80. But the syndicate afterwards decided it would be to their advantage to declare the old contract off, and named 70 as the price at which they would take the bonds.

Woerishoffer said nothing; but cable messages passed between him and the English and German security holders ; and before the New York syndicate was prepared for his campaign, he had corraled in the United States Trust Company more than a majority of the bonds the syndicate were after. Then he informed the gentlemen who had insisted that 80 was too high that, inasmuch as their big foreclosure scheme depended on having the control of these bonds, they would have to pay 100, and he did not let a bond go under par. About $6,000,000 of bonds were involved in the deal. It made Woerishoffer famous in Germany and in London, as well as in New York.

It was he who conceived the scheme of building the Denver & Rio Grande Railroad, which he pushed to completion, and realized large profits for himself and friends.

When the stock was quoted above 110, the Company had a most brilliant outlook, and the public was inveigled into the purchase of long stock which he and his friends held, and a large line of shorts.

He then began the bear campaign on this specialty, and is supposed to have covered some stock as low as 40, realizing immense profits on both sides of the deal.

It was Woerishoffer, too, who pricked the famous Northern Pacific bubble which was inflated to such size and gorgeousness, that men of millions bowed to it. He had been a bull on the Villard stocks until prices had advanced out of all proportion to their intrinsic value. Then he sold out, turned to the short side, and got the appellation of " The Great Bear, Ursa Major."

Woerishoffer declared that the earnings of the Northern Pacific and the Oregon Companies did not warrant the fancy price at which their stocks were quoted ; and he openly sold the whole line short. Arguments having no weight, it was determined to whip him into line, and a syndicate was formed to buy up 100,000 shares to squeeze him out of the way.

The financial powers, like D. O. Mills, Drexel, Morgan & Co., and others of influence, were with Villard. Practically, he had to face them single-handed. His own friends assured him he was atop of a volcano.

The syndicate put in its work and bought 20,000 of the 100,000 shares. Still Woerishoffer did not scare worth a cent. Then with a rush they bid for the other 80,000 shares. Their order was filled. Woerishoffer's brokers filled it with stock bought for that special purpose.

It was a dazed syndicate that met afterwards to talk matters over. But not so dazed as they became soon after when the Street began to wake up to the true inwardness of the situation, and the astute financiers found themselves involved in a panic, with the prices of their sugar-coated stocks tumbling down, down, until Woerishoffer had cleared millions of dollars.

Woerishoffer was not always a bear; he was just as ready to turn bull when he saw great opportunities on that side of the market. He and Cammack were more feared by the big bull leaders than all the other bears on "the Street."

In the Vanderbilt boom of 1885, on the consummation of the "West Shore deal," these two bear leaders were taken into the confidence of Vanderbilt and Pierpont Morgan and let into their scheme. This was an adroit move to make allies, and checkmate the most formidable opposition they would otherwise have had to encounter.

Cammack and Woerishoffer covered their shorts and went heavily long of the market. In the 30 points' rise which followed both made immense profits. Woerishoffer's was said to have been $2,000,000.

H. N. Smith was left out of the deal, and after a small advance he went heavily short of the Vanderbilt, Granger, and other stocks. The result was that Smith went under, in the fall of 1885, for over $1,000,000, and carried the house of William Heath & Co. down in the crash with him.

At one time Woerishoffer was short of Lackawanna and S. V. White heavily long of it. Circumstances favored a big decline in the coal stocks and White wanted to get out. He knew if it became bruited about that he was throwing over his long stock, all the bears in "the Street" would jump on it and the price would drop rapidly.

"Lack." was White's pet specialty, and the public knew it. They knew he made the bears climb for it when opportunity offered for a corner. Hence they did not fear short sales of it, but did fear liquidation.

So White had his stock sold through the bear house of Woerishoffer instead of selling it directly from his own. It was said that 80,000, equivalent to 40,000 full shares, was so sold in one day, without much appreciable effect on the price. White, it was reported, cleared $1,000.000.

The public believed it was short stock Woerishoffer & Co. were selling. When it became known, a day or two after, that it was long stock, sold by the chief bull in it, the price dropped like lead.

No business is more heartless than stock speculation, yet Woerishoffer's generosity was proverbial. His clerks were the envy of every office in "the Street." He spent thousands of dollars every month in helping other men.

At his death he was practically the owner of over 20 seats in the Stock Exchange—worth at least $25,000 a piece. These all went to their present owners as out and out gifts to young brokers whom he had found faithful to his interest.

On Christmas, 1885—and it was not exceptional—he distributed one thousand dollar checks in his offices, gave District Messenger boys twenty dollar and fifty dollar greenbacks, and sent a handsome $500 horse as a present to the cabby who drove him up and down town daily.

He was one of the very few favorites of fortune. All his money was made by his own exertions— and made in Wall Street.

POOR VS. RICH.

Woerishoffer's generosity was exceptional among Wall Street men.

The selfishness of the very rich, and the open-handed liberality of people of moderate means, and the very poor, was never more strikingly illustrated than in the popular contributions to the " World Pedestal Fund " for the erection of a fitting resting place for the great Bartholdi Statue, "Liberty Enlightening the World."

The freedom-loving people of France contributed of their means to build, and the patriotic Bartholdi nearly bankrupted himself to complete his conception of this famous statue and make it a free gift to our great Republic.

A committee of millionaires, bankers, capitalists and men of high standing had long before been organized to receive subscriptions from other people. But precious few of them were willing to go deep down into their own pockets for substantial tokens of their appreciation of the great gift and to set an example of patriotism.

To provide a pedestal and have it completed in time became a question of honor.

The time was approaching for the free transport of the " Goddess ;" by courtesy of the French Government, on one of its own war ships.

A hundred thousand dollars was needed to complete the pedestal. The money bag committee gave up the task in despair, and proclaimed their inability to raise the money.

Then it was that the Hon. Joseph Pulitzer, editor of the *World*, took up the matter with the determination of raising the money forthwith by popular subscription.

Mr. Pulitzer headed the list with $1,000: Pierre Lorrilard, the millionaire tobacconist, followed with another $1,000.

Among Wall Street men, Hon. R. P. Flower gave $650, and Henry Clews gave a handsome contribution. But other than these, Wall Street was hardly a factor in the growth of the fund.

The real patriotism of the American people showed itself grandly in contributions from those in very moderate circumstances; from laboring men and women ; from poor clerks, shop girls, and children in the public schools. Even the newsboys and boot-blacks on the streets contributed pennies from their rags and penury, until in a few months the fund had swelled to the magnificent sum of $106,000, and represented about 120,000 individual contributors.

CHAPTER XII.

SHORT SALES DANGEROUS.

AS long as margin gambling in stocks is the rule the bears are useful as well as the bulls.

The former work to ascertain the vulnerable points in the management of the railway companies. The greater the weakness they discover the more favorable their opportunity.

The professional bears act intelligently on the information they have obtained. They first sell large lines of short stock at the highest prices. Then they begin to expose the real, or apparent rottenness they have discovered, sell more stocks and hammer down the market.

Speculators on weak margins are the first to take alarm and get out, or are wiped out.

When investors have become frightened into liquidation, the bears can stop selling. Prices decline without their help by force of the reams upon reams of stocks pressed on the market for sale. This gives the wise bruins the opportunity to buy in stocks at low prices to cover their shorts and take their profits.

But all this time a class of people have been buying the stocks on the way down. Many buy only to throw their stocks over again at a loss. Others who have bought after a big decline have an object in view.

If the bears are too greedy, have overstayed their market, and stocks have become concentrated in the hands of strong manipulating bulls, the bears are not unfrequently caught napping and lose all their advantage.

The bulls form pools and suddenly put up prices. The bears are squeezed, cornered and made to climb, at advancing prices, to recover the stocks they sold. Obstinate bruins, who hold out, are made to pay a heavy loaning rate from day to day, and the result is often a big loss instead of a profit.

It is the concentration of stocks in strong hands and the cohesion among bulls and bull pools that makes short sales, at times, as dangerous as dynamite.

COMPARATIVE SAFETY.

When prices are high the bears sell stocks as feelers of the market. If things favor the bulls they cover quickly at minimum losses and bide their time.

After an advance of 20, 30, or 40 per cent. from the bottom of a previous decline, the chances are nine out of ten that prices will go down rather than go up. The bears count on this and aim to be in the swim when the right time comes.

The bulls, with no opposition to encounter,

would inflate prices prodigiously beyond real intrinsic value. When a great speculative craze is on, the outsiders always come in at the top, and push prices still higher by wild purchases. This is the opportunity of the inside bulls to sell out at enormous profits and turn to the bear side.

The public always " get left," and get left all the worse if they follow their banker's advice to "hold on " from top figures. It was all planned in advance that the public were to take the losses while the insiders got away with the profits.

When stocks have become widely distributed in the hands of the general public all over the country, there is, and can be, no concentration, no cohesion and no defense against the destruction of values by the bears, who have everything their own way. They are in clover and can gorge them- selves with honey. The bees, who fret and fume at their losses, cannot even turn and sting their tormentors until such time as prices get low enough to tempt others to purchase for an advance.

It is the wide distribution of stocks in weak hands that makes short sales comparative safe.

An experienced broker, speaking of the danger of shorting the market, told the writer " He had seen all of the great bears, from Daniel Drew down, go under in irretrievable ruin, except W. R. Travers and Addison Cammack."

The broker might also have excepted Charles F. Woerishoffer, the greatest bear of them all,

since Drew's time.   Woerishoffer took terrific
risks, but died in the very zenith of success. Had
he lived and continued his speculative career, he
would have belied all the traditions and antece-
dents of " the Street " had he, too, not been swept
under by a financial whirlwind.

Cammack, while a bold operator, is cautious and
wary, and probably never took half the risks
Woerishoffer was accustomed to.

CHAPTER XIII.

WALL STREET VICISSITUDES.

TO illustrate the hold which Wall Street has on those who have once become its votaries: Men are subject through years of varying fortunes to vicissitudes from which one would think they would be glad to escape. Perhaps one out of ten thousand begins with almost nothing and becomes a millionaire, and, not satisfied, goes on until once more he is as poor as when he began.

One man came to New York in 1864, and was drawn into speculative enterprises. He was swamped in the Fort Wayne corner, and left entirely without means.

Necessity prompted him to open an office, and attempt what was then called a curbstone brokerage business. Subsequently he joined the open Board of Brokers. It was before the time of a ticker service, and he was the first to inaugurate the system of furnishing quotations to prominent operators by means of pads. In this way he secured the patronage of leading speculators like Daniel Drew and Henry Keep.

He became in time a great banker and the confidential broker of Jay Gould, " Jim " Fisk and others, and was prominent in the " Black Friday " operations in 1873.

His activity, industry and thorough integrity gained him a numerous clientele, and for many years thereafter he was intrusted with some of the most important transactions made in the " Street." It was well understood that neither for fear nor favor could any information be obtained from him by even his most valuable customers as to the operations he might be conducting for others.

To the implicit confidence in his integrity his success was attributed. His house became one of the best known on the Street, and he had branch offices at both London and Paris.

In the great boom of 1885, based on the " West Shore deal," almost all the big operators, except Cammack and Woerishoffer, and the whole Street were in the dark as to the great movement inaugurated by the late W. H. Vanderbilt and J. Pierpont Morgan.

The banker's office became the headquarters of the bears, who put out large lines of shorts, in blissful ignorance that the rise had only just began.

As prices were pushed up and kept on the advance, this house, true to the interest of its customers, held on, in hopes the boom would exhaust itself. But the sequel proved that their own margins and that of their largest customer were exhausted.

The failure of the house was inevitable, and it came in October. The cause was ascribed to the heavy short interest they were carrying for a large bear operator, who got into them, in Wall Street phrase, to the extent of over a million dollars.

Although it was known that this house was notoriously short of stocks, their failure was entirely unexpected, and excited astonishment.

The banker was arrested under proceedings instituted by one of his principal creditors for the recovery of nearly half a million dollars. Exorbitant bail was required, which he was unable to furnish, and he was committed to Ludlow Street Jail, where he remained two or three months. Then the bail was reduced to a reasonable figure, sureties were obtained and he was released.

In the days of his prosperity this man had numerous and powerful friends, but in adversity they all left him. His health was impaired by long confinement, his heart broken by the collapse of his fortune, the desertion of friends, and the troubles in which his fidelity to his customers had entangled him. He died the next Spring of disease aggravated by mental and pecuniary troubles.

In his halcyon days he was a live lion in finance, in adversity he was but as a dead dog.

The banker had a costly residence on Fifth Avenue, an elegant chateau in France, and could have retired any time within a few years of his failure, with probably a million of dollars or more.

" What's this nigger doing in my pew?"

The banker had driven down to his fashionable church from his fashionable brown-stone house in a fashionable street, and as he sauntered up the aisle, escorted by the sexton, that was what he said to him as he saw a well dressed colored man praying with bowed head, in his softly cushioned pew.

" He's a nigger, to be sure," whispered the fawning sexton, as he opened the door of the pew, " but he's worth a cold half million."

" Introduce me to the gentleman," instantly responded the banker ; " I shall be happy to know him."

That is Wall Street all over.

The god of Wall Street is Mammon ; money is its idol.   Men bow down in homage to the "Golden Calf."   In no other place—in no other business is the world so cold, cynical and heartless in the presence of misfortune.

MORALITY, BULLS VS. BEARS.

The general disposition is to regard the misfortunes of a bear operator as a just punishment for his method of dealing. This is absurd, for the bulls are just as culpable in their methods to filch money away from other people as are the bears.

The bear is the conservator of the stock market.

He acts as the governor of the steam engine, and lifts the safety valve when the steam gets too high.

It is his pleasure and practice to analyze values; to restrain the propensity of the bull to look at everything through a magnifier; to counsel caution and to discover the two sides that exist to everything, even to a railroad company's statements.

More important still, when the bulls have overloaded and the market has become blind drunk with high prices, it is the bear who steps in and prevents the panic which would ensue at an attempt to realize profits.

He slowly prepared for what he saw must occur from the mad speculation going on, by selling as prices advanced, and then when there is no one else to buy, he checks the downward movement by buying what would otherwise be unsalable, thus saving many a speculator from absolute ruin and many a money lender from being compelled to become the owner of the securities on which he had loaned money.

It is not uncommon to hear the bull speculator denounce the practice of the bear in selling that which he does not own ; but it is difficult to see wherein this is worse than for the bull to buy that which he cannot pay for.

The bulk of all transactions in stocks are made on margins. If a rise in price follows a purchase, the buyer takes advantage of it and makes money, but if a severe decline occurs and more margin is not forthcoming, that which he has already deposited to secure his broker is wiped out, and another lamb is slaughtered.

The bulls sometimes resort to the trick of manipulating a scarcity. of stock in the loan room. This is done to carry the idea that there is a large short interest out, in hopes it will induce purchases.in anticipation of prices being put up on a squeeze of the bears. Under cover of such buying they will sell out, and leave their dupes in the lurch. The whole thing is a cheat. There is no big short interest. Stocks are plenty to go around and to spare, except for their trickery.

Wall Street is full of mines and countermines, traps and drag-nets to catch suckers. The dabbler is in a strait betwixt Scylla and Charybdis, and in danger of being wrecked whichever way he turns. Between the traps of the bulls and those of the bears there is no choice but to keep out of both, unless one buys good stocks at a reasonable price, pays for them, and is able to hold on to them for years for results, if necessary.

DANGEROUS STOCKS TO SHORT.

Stocks which have a comparatively small capitalization are particularly dangerous, for the reason that the floating stock is more easily corraled and a corner effected.

The Long Island Railroad is capitalized at $10,000,000. Nobody ever hears of the bears selling that stock short. The reason is, the stock is concentrated in a few strong hands, and it can be cornered quickly and the price run up at a jump from par to $1,000 a share, or any other figure.

Pacific Mail has a stock capital of $20,000,000 par value. It is very hazardous to go short of it unless the stock is widely distributed.

Delaware, Lackawanna and Western is a half share stock. Its par is 50, and its capital is $26,200,000. This stock was formerly the great objective point for bear assaults, for the reason that it then made no public statements, and speculators had to grope in the dark as to its real condition and value.

It has paid dividends, then passed them, and then resumed their payment again. From 1882 to 1885 it paid 8 per cent. per annum. Since then it has paid 7 per cent. Its price from 1880 to the present time has ranged between $68\frac{1}{2}$ and $150\frac{1}{4}$ per full share.

From fifteen to twenty millions of this stock is generally held closely by investors for the dividends, while the balance is floating on the Street, the football of speculation.

It was very easy for bull capitalists to buy up the floating stock, when the bears were heavily short, and effect a corner.

In 1884 the pool in Lackawanna put up the price from 114¼ to 133⅜ "regular." In the height of the squeeze a loaning rate of 4 per cent., or $4 per full share per day, was exacted. So large was the short interest and so eager were the bears to recover the stock they had sold, that they run the prices up on themselves from 133⅜ "regular," to 139½ for "cash" stock for immediate delivery.

Union Pacific has a stock capital of $60,868,500 par. When this stock was paying 7 per cent. dividends probably fifty millions was held by investors. The balance was floating on the Street. It was not an easy matter to corner it. Still it has been cornered, and a loaning rate of ⅛ or ¼ per cent. per day imposed.

Western Union Telegraph has a par capital of $80,000,000, and it is plain to see that it would require a very powerful combination of capital to buy up control and corner it.

This stock has the reputation of having been immensely watered. It used to be charged, again and again by the bears, that the whole plant, wires, poles, electrical instruments and all could be duplicated for $20,000,000.

THE GREAT NORTHWEST CORNER.

The preferred stock of the Chicago and Northwestern is entitled to 7 per cent. dividends before the common stock can get anything. For several years both classes of stock were paying 7 per cent., and accumulating a surplus. " The cutting of the Northwest melon " in the division of this surplus as extra dividends became a standing joke, and was used as an argument to bull the stock.

The difference in price, at market, between the preferred and common stock is usually from 15 to 30 per cent.

In October, 1872, Northwest common ranged in price from 68½ to 83⅝, and the preferred from 84¾ to 90.

In November of that year occurred the great Northwest corner, in which the common stock was put up from 77¾ to $230 a share, and probably a very high loaning rate imposed on it.

During the squeeze the highest price of the preferred stock was only 102. One prominent bear, who was heavily short of the common, attempted to make his deliveries in preferred stock, which was refused. He had to dance to anything but a merry tune in settling up his contracts. In December following the price of Northwest common dropped back to 90 and 81½.

THE HARLEM CORNER.

In 1863 Harlem stock ranged at all prices from 27½ to $179 a share.

In 1864 Commodore Vanderbilt put up the price until in June it was held at $285 a share, and did not appear in the market quotations for a long time afterwards.

8

The Fort Wayne corner occurred in April, 1864, when the price was put up to 152⅝. The highest average price for that year was 116⅛ and the lowest 98¾ per share.

THE GAME OF CHANCE.

Stocks are always dear to the outside public when prices are low and distrust prevails. If they are bound to speculate, this is the very time when they ought to buy for a "long pull." But they have no confidence and will not come in.

When a great movement has been projected, and the bubble has become inflated near its utmost tension, then it is that stocks look cheap. People are imbued with the belief that the extent of the rise has no limit. They rush in to buy and are supplied by the insiders, who have planned for just such a consummation. The result is they get left. Twenty, thirty or forty per cent. margins are wiped out. Or, if financially strong, they have to wait years, perhaps, for another boom to come round to let them out whole.

The saying, "A fool is born every minute," is said to have originated with one of the most prominent operators in Wall street. Certain it is that a new crop of fools is always counted upon and seldom fails to respond to the allurements offered.

The position of those who buy stocks near the top of a boom was never better illustrated than in the " Wall Street " column of the *Evening Telegram* of November 21, 1885. Speaking of the great rise based on the " West Shore deal," it says :

" To attempt to reason on the present phase of speculation in Wall Street is futile. It must be taken for just what it is, a simple credulity that to buy to-day, no matter what insures a profit, all the greater the longer a sale is deferred.

People buy stocks to-day with the same unwavering faith with which a 'darkey' invests the products of a day's boot-shining in 4–11–44, and with about the same substantial grounds for calculating on a profit on his venture.

It is splendid sport as long as it holds out. No one suffers : every one with sufficient courage to take a ' flier ' gains. The bears are living on last year's nuts, or sucking their paws for such nourishment as they may afford. Seats at the Stock Exchange are rising in value. The nearly famished brokers of a year ago are waxing fat and saucy. Diminished bank accounts are growing plethoric again. The pleasant bleat of the sagacious lamb is heard as a sort of chorus to the clink of gold as he counts over his profits and says to himself, ' This is no vision of fancy. This sweet clover and that high grass have come to stay. I shall soon have as much fat on my ribs and wool on my back as will make me comfortable, so buy me a thousand more of anything,'

and his broker pockets the $125 commission and
the lamb has pledged another hostage in the
hands of chance.

True, this state of things may change. Similar
conditions have existed before this, and have
changed, and, strange to say, the sagacious lamb
has not foreseen it. He has almost invariably
been caught in deshabille, so to speak, and the
joyful bleat is changed to a pitiful moan. His
broker ignores him if he is not left in his debt ;
his friends jeer at him ; and though Sterne says
that the 'Lord tempers the wind to the shorn
lamb,' one has only to look around Wall Street
after a panic, to see how false the saying is—for
the Lord don't do anything of the kind. On the
contrary, the bears come out of the woods, as
they did in Elijah's time, and treat the lambs as
in those days they treated the wicked boys, with
the unanimous Christian verdict of " Served him
right.

    *   *   *   *   *   *

The result of an attempt to liquidate these accounts could not fail to be disastrous, and once
again the voice of the mourner will be heard
in the land—the lambs weeping for their profits,
and 'refusing to be comforted because they are
not.'

The projectors of this movement, so unprece-
dentedly successful, have realized on their ventures beyond question, and now stand aside to

watch the bursting of a bubble which has expanded far beyond their most sanguine expectations.

When this has taken place, and the smoke cleared from the field of battle, so that the dead can be counted and the wounded placed in hospital, it will be in order for new deals to be organized, when, with new scenery, dresses and decorations, the same old play will be revived—or, more correctly, the same old contest be fought over. Unlimited capital, skill in manipulation, plausible pretexts with just enough truth at the bottom to swear by, respectable names to indorse projects of promise rather than of performance on the one side and blooming verdancy on the other, and the same result—slaughtered lambs, not forced to the shambles, but coaxed in, lured to their destruction by those whose colossal fortunes and princely edifices are cemented by the blood of these "innocents.

They cannot say that they have not been warned. 'They have heard it, but they heeded not.'"

CHAPTER XIV.

WALL STREET SPECULATORS.

JASON, of old, sailed along the shores of Far Cathay and the ancient Colchis in search of the Golden Fleece, but could never find it.

The adventurers who navigate the dangerous coasts of Wall Street on a similar mission are scarcely more successful.

They number a vast multitude of both sexes, and come from all quarters of the compass. Every business day, between 9 and 10 o'clock A. M., the Brooklyn, Staten Island and Jersey ferry boats, the elevated trains and horse cars are full of them.

They come from way off on Long Island, from far away in New Jersey, from the Hudson River towns and villages and south-western Connecticut; from anywhere, within two or three hours' ride of the Metropolis, by fast steamers and railway trains.

Broadway and the adjacent streets are alive with them, all making for a common goal, their bankers' and brokers' offices. Dives comes down in his private carriage, or in a hired coupe, away from the common herd.

Inside the offices they feel at home, inspect the Wall Street papers and news tape for the latest information. They consult their brokers or wrangle with each other on the prospects of the day; for there are both bulls and bears in the same office.

At 10 o'clock they congregate around the ticker, eager for the opening quotations on which to base their orders for the morning. They hang over the indicator by the hour and scan every fluctuation. Business lasts from 10 A. M. to 3 P. M., continuously.

The tape speculators are there as regularly as the bankers, brokers and clerks. In aggregate numbers, they would make up an army. These, however, constitute but a fraction of another class, who are seldom seen on Wall Street, but who send their orders by post and telegraph from up town and from all over the country.

Those who manipulate the market for sure results are doubtless happy over the boodle they have drawn into their coffers by trickery and craft.

The bankers and brokers are happy in proportion to the frequency and size of their commissions.

But the life of an outside speculator has far, far more of misery than of happiness.

The feeling is one of ecstasy to him who sees his ventures rolling up a profit of $500 or $1,000 on each 100 shares he has out. If he is wise, he will seize it. If too greedy, and he waits, the substance he coveted vanishes like a shadow, and perhaps engulfs his margins.

Prices advance or decline by fractions of eighths. Each $\frac{1}{8}$ represents a loss or gain of $12.50 on 100 shares. In an active market prices jump up or down by quarters, halves or whole points at a time.

If a man buys or sells short 100 shares, and the market goes his way 1 per cent., and he closes the deal there, his broker takes $25 for his commission; the balance, $75, is his profit, less interest, if any, for carrying. If the market goes against him 1 per cent., and he closes the deal at that loss, he is out of pocket $125, of which $100 is loss on the stock and $25 commissions on the turn ; in addition, he is minus all interest that may accrue for carrying the stock for him if he is long, or of any loaning rate imposed if he is short.

Speculators may be divided into two classes, those who deal for a "long pull" and big profits of from 5 to 20 per cent., and those who operate for scalping profits of fractions or a point or two.

The first are like the disciples of Isaak Walton, who put out their lines and wait patiently for hours for a respectable 3 or 5 pound bass to take the hook.

Those who go in for a long pull wait days, weeks and months for results At times they may have many hundreds of dollars profit in sight. They want to do better and wait. A sudden change comes over the market, the profits vanish, big losses accrue to those on weak margins. Those who are strong hold on and wait weeks and months longer for the market to come around their way again.

The other class who go in for " short turns" are like the fellows who fish for minnows at the creek, for the fun of pulling out the little fish as fast as they can bait the hook and throw it in.

They try to buy at the bottom of the daily slumps and sell out on the bulges, at profits of $50, $100, or $200. The market may be run in a groove for days at a time with uniform fluctuations up and down, perhaps two or three times a day. This is a good traders' market while it lasts. They get in and out with several small profits of $100, more or less, daily. Then prices are suddenly moved up or down, to a much higher or lower level, generally when they are on the wrong side. They lose all their profits, if not their margins.

It is the fate of most speculators to get in wrong at least three times out of five. The news, gossip and often false rumors circulated have a subtle, undefinable influence over the mind, perverting cool judgment and discretion, and leading fools into a trap intentionally set for them.

The hook is baited. The anglers are cunning and powerful. They move the market at will.

They play with their game as a cat plays with a mouse. When the time is ripe, and there is a good run of suckers, the net is drawn in and the profits secured.

Success is everything to a man in Wall Street. The prosperous gambler is confident, self-satisfied and don't care a fig for the good opinion of anybody.

The better class of people whose avocations are above taint or suspicion of gambling, look on the business of stock speculation as disreputable and demoralizing. They soon come to know the Wall Street men who pass, at certain hours, daily on their way to and from "the Street." Speculators know this and also the opinion with which they are regarded.

Unlucky speculators, outside the banker-broker offices, often have the furtive look and exhibit the hang-dog feeling of a sneak thief, or a sheep stealer. They are Wall Street lamb and they know it, and they think everybody else knows it too.

HAPPINESS.

About four years ago a speculator got a straight tip of a good thing to happen in Northwest common. Next morning he ordered his brokers to buy him 1,000 shares of it at the-opening. They did so. Northwest advanced, and before closing had gone up over ten points. Then he ordered the stock sold, which was done at a clear net profit of $10,000. All made within five hours.

MISERY.

Of all the cliqued stocks none were more dangerous to go short of than Delaware, Lackawanna and Western. It was equally dangerous to buy, even on 30 per cent. margins, unless bought under par. Its fluctuations for eleven months in 1884–5 were nearly 50 per cent., and this too was brought about more by artifice than natural causes.

In January, 1885, its price was down around 82. A speculator bought 200, equivalent to 100 full shares, at about 83. It advanced, and at $88\frac{1}{2}$ he took profits and sold 200 short. Still the price advanced, and at $95\frac{1}{2}$ he sold another 200 short to average down. The price kept going up with occasional reactions until in December it reached 135.

Now when a stock goes "ex-dividend" the price drops off just the extent of the dividend. When Lackawanna paid two per cent. quarterly, if the price at market was 120 with the dividend on, it would be 118 the moment it went ex-dividend, and be subject to fluctuations from that price.

If a bear is short of a stock when it goes ex-dividend, he has to pay the dividend to the man he last borrowed the stock of, to keep good his delivery, when the dividend was on it.

In April, 1885, the bear before mentioned had to pay $400 dividend on his 400 half shares. And in July he had to pay another $400 dividend on the same.

In the meantime there had been a squeeze in it and he had to pay a loaning rate of from $\frac{1}{64}$ to $\frac{1}{8}$ per day, and on one day it was one per cent., then the stock became easy and the loaning rate ceased.

Altogether, at one time, he stood for a loss of over $5,000 on stock, dividends and loaning rates.

The October dividend was reduced to $1\frac{3}{4}$ or 7 per cent. per annum. He escaped the payment of this by covering his shorts. Whether he caught on short again is a matter of conjecture.

Another bear sold 200 Lackawanna short at 88 ; 200 more at 90 ; 200 at 92 ; 200 at 95, and 200 at 98. Anybody can imagine the loss he stood for on his shorts with the loaning rates and dividends he had to pay.

One bull bought 500 shares of Texas and Pacific stock in 1881 at 65 per share. It declined, but he held on until 1884 and then sold it for $15 a share. His loss was $25,000 on stock, $125 on commissions, and he lost all income for about two and a half years on the $32,500 his stock cost him.

Another bull bought 100 shares Bloomington in 1882 at $44\frac{1}{2}$, and in 1883 he bought 100 shares Oregon Trans-Continental at $55\frac{5}{8}$. Prices went down on him until in 1884 the lowest price was 9 and $6\frac{1}{4}$ per share, respectively. He has the stock yet, and the highest price reached since has been $28\frac{1}{8}$ for Bloomington and 38 for O. T. Neither stock pays any income.

Instances like these could be multiplied *ad libitum*, where people, who bought stocks at high prices years ago, are still holding on to their hundreds and thousands of shares and waiting for the coming of the millennium.

The widest fluctuations of any one stock in 1884 was in Bankers' and Merchants' Telegraph. In February the highest price was $126.75 per share, and in October following only $1 per share.

The question arises: Why will people speculate at such fearful risks?

The answer is, that most of them were first lured in on a booming market. They could and did snatch frequent profits by buying on the reactions and selling out on the rallies. When the gambling instinct is once aroused and gratified, the result is they become the slaves of infatuation, delusion, credulity and greed. The business has a snake-like fascination which few of its victims can resist, as long as they can raise a margin to continue it.

When they cannot handle a respectable 100 share lot they go over to the Consolidated Stock and Petroleum Exchange and operate in ten share lots, on margins of from $20 to $100. From this they can drift down to the bucket shops and continue the game as long as they can raise, borrow or beg $5, the lowest limit.

As long as men of wealth and standing, senators, congressmen, ex-cabinet ministers, state officials, deacons, church wardens, vestrymen, Sunday-school teachers, and even stray clergymen come into the Street to speculate on margins, just so long will the business have an appearance of respectability and legitimacy. Legitimate in law it is, but morally it is all wrong, and leads to untold hardship and misery, not alone to the guilty, but to multitudes of innocent people.

The Rev. W. H. Milburn, the blind Chaplain of the House of Representatives, on March 22, 1886, "devoted his opening prayer to an invocation to God to rid the land of gamesters, whether in cards, dice, chips, stocks, wheat, bucket shops or boards of trade, and to lead the people to know that money making other than by the sweat of the face was contrary to His laws."

"On motion of Mr. Butterworth, of Ohio, seconded by Mr. Weaver, of Iowa, this prayer was ordered to be inserted in the minutes."

BANKERS' PRECAUTIONS.

In many offices tissue letter press copies of correspondence received or sent out, written orders to buy or sell, and bills of purchases and sales are taken. Orders in pencil are often preserved; all this as a precaution against future trouble. A client may be directly led into a bad scrape and a heavy loss through the damnable influence brought to bear to get him in for the sake of commissions. But this influence is oral, often between man and man. The customer is generally alone. He has no redress. If disposed to fight, the oral influences don't count against the fac-simile copies of his letters, orders, bills of purchase or sale, and every clerk in the office ready to back up the banker and broker in a court of law.

CHAPTER XV.

GREAT SWINDLES, REMOTE AND RECENT. MISSISSIPPI SCHEME.

IN 1679 La Salle discovered the great district northwest of the lower confluence of the Mississippi River, known as Louisiana, and which became the property of France.

In 1717 John Law, a celebrated financier and native of Edinburgh, established a bank in Paris, by royal authority. The stock was 1,200 shares of 3,000 livres each, which soon bore a premium.

This bank became the office for all public receipts, and the same year there was annexed to it a Mississippi company which had grants of land in Louisiana and was expected to realize immense sums by planting and commerce.

Law's famous scheme was a plan for relieving the bankrupt French treasury by parcelling out the Valley of the Mississippi among stock jobbers and commercial gamblers.

Thousands of colonists were sent out and a mania for speculation seized all classes of French society.

In 1718 the bank was declared a royal institution, and its shares rose to twenty times their original value.

The bubble burst in 1720 and the shares sank in value as rapidly as they had risen, occasioning widespread financial distress and bankruptcy.

Law fled from the wrath of the people, who were left in worse poverty and misery than ever.

SOUTH SEA BUBBLE.

In the year 1720 the South Sea Company, a trading corporation of London, having exclusive privileges, offered to buy up the government annuities with a view to the reduction of the public debt.

The proposal was accepted and great numbers of the people hastened to invest in the stock of the Company, which rose to an extraordinary premium.

It was a stupendous stock jobbing scheme, and after running its course a few months the great bubble burst.

Merchants, lawyers, clergy, physicians and others passed from their dreams of fabulous wealth, and from their wonted comforts into penury. Some died of broken hearts, others removed to remote parts of the world and never returned.

It was characterized at that time as "the most enormous fabric of national delusion ever raised amongst an industrious and prudent people."

PANIC OF 1837.

New York in the years 1835-6 was the scene of wild and, for that time, colossal speculations. All kinds of business and commerce was stimulated to its utmost tension. In 1837 occurred the most disastrous commercial panic ever known on the Western Continent. About 60 banks with over $150,000,000 of liabilities were engulfed in ruin. Merchants and storekeepers of all kinds failed right and left until the total indebtedness was between $400,000,000 and $500,000,000. It became a standing joke that the average basis of settlement on this grand aggregate was but one penny on the dollar. Almost everybody was in debt to somebody else, and was suing or being sued, until almost this entire immense sum was eaten up in law costs.

THE EMMA MINE.

The Emma Silver Mining Company originated in London, way back in the fifties or sixties. The mine itself was situated in the Cottonwood Cañon, Utah, about 25 miles from Salt Lake City.

The property was capitalized at £1,000,000 sterling, and half the stock was offered to the public at par in £20 shares. The other half was to be retained for nine months in expectation of a high premium on rich developments.

The mine proved productive, and the last half of the stock was readily sold at a big advance. Twenty-two dividends, the last in 1864, were paid, amounting to $1,394,400. With the passing of the dividends, the stock rapidly declined, and almost went out of sight as a speculation. The value of bullion it had produced was $5,240,000.

In 1871 the mine passed into other hands, and a new company was formed, comprising both English and American capitalists. The chief promoter of the Company was a noted Englishman, who, in the prospectus, included the name of a prominent U. S. official as a drawing card.

It afterwards transpired that the said public official was induced to take stock and become a director by the present to him of 500 shares for the use of his name, and a salary of $2,500 a year, which all the directors were to get.

An expert had been employed to visit the mine, and in his report said: "There were several facts which in his opinion established beyond all reasonable doubt the conclusion that the Emma Mine was a true mineral vein of great power, and placed it in the category of the great mines of the world. And that ore to the value of several millions of dollars had already been removed from it."

A large amount of stock was floated at £20 a share. The London promoter of the scheme was paid £100,000. An American banking house was paid £25,000 for the use of their name, and the mine expert received £9,000 or £10,000 for making his favorable report.

Shareholders, both English and American, thought our Government was backing the enterprise, because the United States public official's name was in the prospectus as a Director.

Dividends were paid for thirteen months consecutively, at $1\frac{1}{2}$ per cent. per month, until December, 1872.

Great numbers of people took the bait, and bought at high prices. The stock was boomed up to £32 per share in May, 1872.

When the dividends ceased, the insiders had sold out and gone short, and the stock had a rapid decline to £1 5s. per share.

The collapse caused great losses and distress to immense numbers of people, afterwards aggravated by assessments on the stock, until at the close of 1874 these levies had reached $1,832,000. The mine had become exhausted long before.

Subsequently the personal property of the Company was sold under execution, issued in favor of an American capitalist, who was a Director of the Company.

In 1875–6 the matter became the subject of Congressional investigation, and resulted in a resolution of censure of the " public official " for having had anything to do with the mine as a Director while discharging the duties of his position as an accredited officer of the Government.

In England the matter was taken up in the House of Commons so far as it related to British subjects.

The developments raised a tremendous breeze

in this country. Many suits grew out of the complications, and efforts were made to implicate the late Hon. James B. McKean, then Chief Justice of Utah, because he could not be used as a pliant tool in the Emma Mine suits that came up before his court.

THE CREDIT MOBILIER.

The American Credit Mobilier, patterned after the French Company of that name, was organized, ostensibly to make loans and aid Construction Companies.

In 1867 the Credit Mobilier Company came under the control of the contractors who were building the Union Pacific Railroad.

Prominent capitalists of New York, Boston and other cities were interested in it.

For a time the Company flourished. About four millions of stock were issued, enormous dividends were paid, and it was made to appear a mine of gold. The value of the stock became greatly inflated, and, as usual, the public grabbed for it, and it became widely distributed.

Its projectors realized fabulous profits selling out on the people. Subsequently the bubble collapsed just as its French prototype had done long before, and just as the South Sea Bubble and Law's scheme had done near the beginning of the eighteenth century. People who had invested their money in it were scooped by the wholesale.

An investigation several years afterwards revealed the fact that not a few Senators and Congressmen were interested and had owned stock in the Company.

Charges and counter-charges were promiscuously made. Recommendations of censure and expulsion were offered.

All this, locking the stable door after the horse had been stolen, did not help the people who had been fleeced to recover their money.

The Credit Mobilier scheme had become so interwoven with the construction of the Union Pacific, and as the building of the railroad was promoted by grants of land and other assistance by Congress, it savored too much of stock jobbery and corruption, that any member of the National Legislature should have had any private interest in either Company.

It was the great scandal of the period and for a long time a stench in the nostrils of the American people.

Suits in connection with the Credit Mobilier have continued to crop out in the Courts even down to a very recent time.

CATTLE RANCHES.

Wall Street men have many irons in the fire outside of stock speculation. Various land and cattle companies have their head-quarters in New York and issue stock of their corporations.

Millions of dollars are invested in sheep and cattle raising in Texas and the western Territories.

The reservations set apart for the exclusive use of the Indians are intruded upon in the red-hot pursuit of wealth.

In 1885 this matter was made the subject of complaint to the Government by Gen. Edward McCook, whereupon President Cleveland issued a proclamation warning the cattlemen to remove with their live stock from the reservations.

The only effect was that they did remove for a time and then came back again. In 1886 the annual " round up " on the ranges proceeded the same as before, and the President's proclamation was ignored.

However, ranges, immense herds, and cowboys are gradually disappearing, and thousand acre stock farms and barbed-wire fences are taking their place.

Even Yellowstone Park was overrun by swarms of greedy speculators. An editorial in the Brooklyn *Eagle* in 1885, discussing this matter, said :

" KEEP THEM OUT OF YELLOWSTONE PARK.

An effort is being made to convert the national property known as Yellowstone Park to private uses. Political and financial pressure can readily be, and perhaps have been, brought to bear on Congress to further the schemes of land grabbers,

hotel builders and railway magnates, who fancy
that in this region are opportunities for the making of big fortunes. Yellowstone Park was set
apart from permanent settlement for the benefit
of the American people and of all other people
who choose to explore it. No spot of earth contains so many scenic beauties, so many wondrous
exhibitions of color, so many phenomena of scien-
tific interest as this reservation. There are snowy
peaks brooding over wide expanses of forest;
cañons cleave the earth to a fearful depth and re-
sound with roar of cataracts plunging into them;
fantastic rock forms, painted in colors of almost
prismatic liveliness, dot the mountain sides; clear
lakes, with flower gemmed banks, gleam in the
valleys; hills of sulphur, dykes of crystallized
basalt and domes of limestone form monuments of
volcanic action, as do the cliffs of sparkling black
glass, as high as the Hudson River Palisades; hot
springs pour from terraces of self-built travertine,
the frets and water growths that face and line
pools rivaling frost work in their delicacy; 'paint
pots' blob and sputter, boiling red .and yellow
slime of sulphurous odor; fumaroles and solfataras
roar and whistle; boiling pools stripe the plains
of sinter with metallic colors, marking their lines
of outflow, and geysers fling their columns 150
feet from earth, shaking the ground with the fury
of their eruptions, charging the winds with clouds
of steam and scaring the elk in the covert with

their hoarse bellowing. There are scenes of more tranquil beauty, also ; grassy plains, slopes commanding prospects of purple mountains, still rivers, and cascades showering in silver sheets into shaded pools. It is a region of wonder and delight, and should inure forever to the people.

To apportion the park among railroad companies that would strip its forests from the hillsides, and to land speculators who would fence in the springs, the geysers and the cañons, peddling admissions thereto, as used to be done at Niagara, would cast disgrace on every official and representative engaged in such an act. It would be simple robbery of the public, as much so as would be the gift of Prospect Park to private corporations, for conversion into stock and lumber yards. Thousands of tourists visit the Yellowstone every Summer for health, pleasure and instruction, and the number is increasing every year.

Speculators and monopolists have already secured possession of vast territory beyond the Mississippi, non-residents owning over 21,000,000 acres, and the farmer and ranchman who wishes to start for himself in a moderate way no longer finds that as easy to do as it was twenty years ago. Should Yellowstone Park be opened, at the instigation of lobbyists who are trying to influence Congress to that end, intending settlers would have little benefit of it. The park cannot be turned into farms, for most of its surface is mountainous, and lifted into plateaus from 3,000 to 8,000 feet above the sea. The climate is therefore chilly, frosts are common in the nights of Summer, and Winter comes early and stays late. The valleys could be used as cattle ranges, but there is richer grass and more abundance along the Yellowstone below the park.

It has been asserted that there is need of a railroad through this region to establish communication between the Northern and Union Pacific lines ; an assertion about as sensible as that would be which should claim that in order to establish connection between Fulton and Court Streets it was necessary to go over the top of the City Hall. The park is sixty miles broad — narrower than the grant that the railroad projectors probably hope to secure—so that is no great hardship on the railroad companies to go on either side of it ; and, as a matter of fact, it would be a difficult thing to push a railroad through this domain, for the mountains form an almost impenetrable barrier. One railroad is already in operation between Helena and Ogden to westward of the park, and that more than suffices for the traffic between the Union and Northern Pacific lines. If it is desired to link them together at another point, the line should be drawn at least 200 miles east ward from the Yellowstone, where there would naturally be more travel and more freighting than among the wild and uninhabited mountains and alkali deserts of Wyoming. There is no excuse for despoiling Yellowstone Park. Keep the vandals and speculators out of it."

CHAPTER XVI.

RAILROAD RIVALRY.

THE stock of many of the old railroads was so largely watered that they were made to pay dividends on a capital of double or treble their actual cost. These corrupt methods were destructive. When they had the whole monopoly of the carrying business, with no competition, they got along famously. But when they had to divide up the business with new competing roads, costing but a fraction of the enormously watered stock of the old companies, then it became difficult to pay interest on bonds and fixed charges and have anything left for dividends.

Thus when the railway lines connecting through from New York to the West were increased from three to seven, it gave rise to cut-rate wars and crippled the earning capacity of all of them.

Then pool partnerships were formed to stop cutting and restore freight rates to a profitable basis. In the end it was found that there was not business enough to go around.

The New York Central & Hudson River Railroad was, in its best days, one of the grandest properties in the country. It had double tracks from New

York to Albany, and was a great four track road through the heart of the State from Albany to Buffalo.

It had the monopoly of a remunerative traffic all along its line. Its allies, the Lake Shore and Michigan Southern, were its feeders in passenger and an enormous through freighting business from Chicago.

The bulk of the products of the great West entering New York for home consumption and export passed over its line. It had no competitor for local traffic from tide water to Lake Erie, except the Erie Canal, and that only for about six months in the year.

It was a solid eight per cent. dividend payer, and so continued even after other lines became sharers in the carrying trade from the West to the seaboard.

About half its stock was held by the greatest capitalist in America, who was as much an autocrat in speculative finance as any despot in the political world, so much so that public opinion and the influence of the press was brought to bear, pointing out the dangers of the concentration of such an enormous monopoly in the hands of any one man.

It was probably the fear of restrictive legislation that induced this capitalist to dispose of the bulk of his holdings of Central Hudson stock that it might become widely distributed. At all events

W. H. Vanderbilt privately sold 250,000 shares to a syndicate in November, 1879, and 100,000 shares more in January following, all of it at about $120 per share, which was from six to nineteen per cent. below the price at market.

Had it been known that such a large amount of stock was for sale, it would have been sold down by the bears, to the demoralization of the whole market. Hence it was sold to a syndicate. They could take time to feed it out at a good profit according to the strength of the market. In the meantime Vanderbilt had immediate relief from the pressure of public opinion, while still virtually controlling the road.

The building of the New York, West Shore and Buffalo Railway, paralleling the Central Hudson road its entire length, was a speculation and a menace. It gave rise to cut rates and a ruinous competition for local business all along the line.

Anything like a remunerative business was out of the question, until the New York Central secured the control of the West Shore under foreclosure proceedings on a majority of the bonds it had bought up.

Thus the new road became saddled on the Central under a lease for 100 years, and it now has to pay four per cent. interest on $50,000,000 of West Shore bonds, and must pay operating expenses, taxes and fixed charges of every kind on both its own and the West Shore before it can pay any dividends on its own stock.

In former years one of the great sources of N. Y. Central's revenue was found in the transportation charges on wheat from the West for export to Europe.

Now the wheat deficit of European nations is largely supplied with the cereal from Russia and India, especially the latter, which can ship its wheat by the short cut through the Suez Canal, and lay it down in the markets of Europe much cheaper than America can.

When there is no export demand for our grain products, all that is not required for home consumption will naturally remain in the granaries of the West, and to that extent be a loss in the freight earnings of the carriers.

Besides this, where the Central Hudson formerly divided freight transportation only with the Erie Canal, it now has to divide up with more than half a dozen different railroads and the water way, all having entrance into the port of New York.

The immediate outlook for anything more than four per cent. dividends on N. Y. Central is not promising. It may eventually pay six per cent. income on its stock, but it will be a long time, if ever, before it can pay eight per cent. again.

LAKE SHORE.

The Lake Shore and Michigan Southern was

almost as valuable as the New York Central until it became paralleled by the New York, Chicago and St. Louis. It was a Vanderbilt road, and an eight per cent. dividend payer until December, 1884, when the dividends were passed and not resumed again until the last quarter of 1886. The highest price of Lake Shore in 1881 was 135$\frac{3}{4}$, and the lowest about 115. Its highest price in 1884 was 104$\frac{3}{4}$, and the lowest 59$\frac{1}{2}$, but it did not reach the bottom of its decline until the Spring or Summer of 1885, when the price went under 51.

NICKEL PLATE.

The building of the New York, Chicago and St. Louis (Nickel Plate) so close alongside the Lake Shore was a fearful blow at the Vanderbilt pride.

The Nickel Plate was the cheapest specimen of a railroad that was ever projected or constructed. It was a speculation and a very brassy concern from the outset. W. H. Vanderbilt made the worst bargain of his life when he bought it. It was the only road called a Vanderbilt property that he ever allowed to go into the hands of a receiver. He could not help it. He was forced to the extremity for his own protection. The cutting out of other interests caused a fearful howl to be set up.

The only advantage he derived by the possession of it was to keep it from destroying the business of the Lake Shore. However, as it was, it destroyed the financial state of the latter road, compelling it to stop dividends for a time. When the Nickel Plate is fully reorganized, the bonds issued will be guaranteed by the Lake Shore and be valuable. But its stock, except for control, will not be worth much.

EFFECT OF VANDERBILT'S DEATH.

W. H. Vanderbilt was a mighty moving power in the stock market. The first effect of the death of such a man naturally excites fear and apprehension that he has left a large line of speculative stocks which may be thrown on the market, causing a severe decline in prices.

He died on the afternoon of December 8, 1885, too late for the news to reach the Stock Exchange before the close of business.

The news was wired all over the country and to Europe. It was expected that a flood of long stock would be thrown on the market by frightened people, with disastrous results on values. Also that the bear operations would add to the demoralization.

At the opening of business next morning the galleries of the Exchange were packed by those eager to witness the first mad rush of the bears to break the market. This had been foreseen : the big bulls had united to sustain prices as a matter of self-preservation.

Somehow not a single private wire in the street was working. The bulk of country selling orders expected were kept out of the market and the bears were handicapped by lack of these reinforcements.

The battle opened at 10 o'clock with a wild rush. The contending factions came together like two thunder clouds followed by a hoarse roar. The bears closed in and drove the bulls back from their positions. This, however, was but temporary. The bulls rallied and bid up prices as fast as the bears offered them down. The skirmish lasted ten minutes, then the bears retired from the contest.

Prices of the general list opened one and two points below the previous day's closing. Lake Shore, as expected, was the pivotal stock, and opened off three per cent. at 85 from 88. The bulls put it up to 86 and kept it around that figure. The chief bull in Lackawanna ran his pet stock up five and a half points above the opening figure.

Drexel, Morgan & Co. bought 25,000 shares in the first flurry, then large buying orders in New York Central came in from London, engineered by Mr. D. P. Morgan, who had just arrived from the Continent.

But for the trick in stopping telegraphic orders to sell, from all over the country, the bulls would have been compelled to buy reams upon reams of country held stock in order to sustain the market.

CHAPTER XVII.

MANIPULATION.

WHEN circumstances are not favorable for a decided advance or decline in prices, the fluctuations of the market are often almost wholly artificial. At such times the "big men" keep prices steady by washes, without accumulating stock, or leave the market to the room traders to operate for scalping profits.

The room traders are their own brokers, and pay no commission, unless on orders executed for them. Each fraction their way on 100 shares shows them a profit in sight of $12.50, and each point $100.

As speculation turns so largely on trickery and artifice, what is to hinder some ten or twenty room traders, more or.less, forming a secret "combine" to put the prices of certain stocks up and down within a range of one or two per cent., and repeat two or three times a day? Two, three, or four different stocks are enough for their purpose. To take the whole list in hand would be too big a job.

They could begin by buying 500 or 1,000 shares each of Union Pacific at, say, 50, Jersey Central at 55, Lackawanna at 130 and St. Paul at 90. All these they might pick up without raising the price, by washing prices back every time the price advanced a fraction or two. Having secured the stock they want, say 2,000 or 4,000 shares, what is to hinder their washing prices up, say, 2 per cent. by 11 o'clock?

Then to sell out and take profits around the top, prices could be kept up on washes until they had sold out and got on the short side 2,000 or 4,000 shares. Then the washing down process could be brought into play, and by 1 o'clock they could cover their shorts and get around on the long side again, 2,000 or 4,000 shares. Then by washing prices up they might sell out and get short again and close out their deals by 3 o'clock, leaving prices to close just about where they opened in the morning. Here would be two deals on the bull side and two on the bear side. With profits of 2 per cent. on each deal, the gain on 2,000 shares would be $4,000 each time—total 4 times, $16,000. If it was 4,000 shares at 2 per cent. on each of the four deals the profits would be $32,000 to divide up among the pool.

But who would be buying all this stock of, or selling it to them? Why, those fellows, the tape speculators, scattered around in a hundred stock houses. Some of them would get out with a little profit, the rest would get left.

Such practices are not given in this work as

actual facts. Outsiders, and even many brokers, are not let into the inner secrets of the board room. But if some of those inside fellows, who operate for their private account, were brought to the confessional they could make surprising revelations.

Certain it is, the market is often made to fluctuate up and down within certain limits, and a class of room traders are known to buy and sell, individually, many hundred shares a day for their private account.

In this connection, a little story may not be out of place to illustrate:

Michael, on his way to church, meets Pat, an unconverted Irishman, who had never been in a church in his life, and persuades Pat to go with him. In the church Pat looks around in open-eyed wonder while Michael proceeds with his devotions. Presently Pat flops down on his knees alongside of Michael and whispers: "This bates the devil." "That is the intintion Pat," says Michael, in the middle of a pater noster.

The point is that the tricks of the stock market "bates the devil," and that seems to be the intention, too, so far as the speculative public who come into it are concerned.

SPECULATIVE CLERKS.

Clerks in brokerage offices are in a very hotbed of temptation. Next to the brokers, executing orders in the board room, they are the class who have the earliest information as to which way the tide is running among the speculators in their own office. For orders executed by the broker are usually sent in immediately, by messenger, to be entered on the books.

All the business is confidential. The clerks must keep the secrets of the office and not reveal the operations of one customer to any of the others.

Some speculators maintain great secrecy as to the side they are operating on and of the stocks they are dealing in. Their deals can only be guessed at. Others are free to let everybody know what they are doing.

In some offices there are large traders, who operate for big stakes. And if most of the other customers are making ventures in the same direction, the cupidity of the clerks is aroused to get in the swim, if they have a little money to put up as margin. $25, $50 or $100 will do for from 20 to 50 shares.

Yet, with all the chances and the insight of what is going on, they are just as unlucky as any other class on the Street. They may hit right for several times in succession. In the end they risk all once too often and are left as bad, or worse off than before.

One young man inherited $20,000. He came in the Street with the idea of making it $100,000.

The usual result followed ; he soon lost it all. He became a clerk and is an impecunious clerk still, living from hand to mouth, always trying his luck when he can raise a 1 per cent. margin on ten or twenty shares, which is often swallowed up within an hour of the venture.

The parents of a clerk in a stock office, on leaving home for a vacation, left $200 with him to pay rent and household expenses during their absence. He got a sure point that a certain stock would have a good rise and bought 100 shares on a two per cent. margin. The "sure point" proved a crooked steer, and his deal was closed out within two hours, with the $200 all " gone where the woodbine twineth."

Another clerk, with a very small margin as a basis, had a great run of luck. Profits accumulated until he had $20,000. Had he been wise and run away, all would have been well. But excited by cupidity to make a great strike, he bought stocks to the full strength of his $20,000 as margin. It happened he bought too high up, for the bears got control of the market and raided values down 15 per cent. in two or three days. The $20,000 vanished like a dream, leaving him to chew the cud of sweet and bitter fancies. He is still trying his luck in a small way and "waiting like Micawber for something to turn up."

As a class the clerks in Wall Street offices are better paid than those in almost any other business.

They are in a dangerous atmosphere of temptation, and few can resist the seductive influences of
their surroundings.   They are thoroughly imbued
with the instinct of the gambler.   The one who
would scruple to match silver dollars, halves or
quarters on the contigency of a certain stock going up or down, would almost be a *rara avis* among
his fellows.

WOMEN SPECULATORS.

People having no actual experience of Wall
Street can have but a faint idea of the extent of
the hallucination which continually draws fresh
grist to the speculative mill.   In effect it is a species of insanity which allures young and old of
both sexes into the maelstrom.   Some come for
excitement, to relieve their minds of other troubles.
All come to try their luck in the race for wealth.

Often fathers and sons, or mothers with a son
or daughter, just taking an eye-opener in the great
world of business, stand side by side at the tickers.
If fortune favors for the moment, they laugh and
cackle and build castles in the air.   More often
they are depressed with gloom, or, if women,
wring their hands in terror as they see their money
disappear.   What a school to initiate the young
into the mysteries of gambling !

A great many offices have a clientele of women
speculators who commence by dealing in 100 share

lots and upwards. Some of the best customers are found in the ranks of the fair sex.

A correspondent of the Brooklyn *Eagle* got the following description from a broker friend:

About ten minutes before the ticker announces the opening of the Exchange her loveliness pops into the private office and reads all the gossip hung upon the hooks. She then seats herself to await the first quotation. In the meantime her vocabulary organs are exercised in discussing the latest move of Jay Gould or the last fluctuation in the coal stocks or the Chicago syndicate. Tick, tick. " My gracious !" she exclaims, "St. Paul, 90½. Close out my short stuff at the market. Telegraph 47¼. Buy me 100 at an eighth. Oh, no, don't. It's an eighth now. Make it at four. Have you got my St. Paul yet ? " She gets it at 90¾, and it immediately declines to 90. Then she becomes angry, and flounces out of the office, only to return inside of half an hour, when she wants to know if that Telegraph was bought at 74. No, it was not, as an eighth was the lowest price touched, and the quotation at the time of her query was 75½. It is not always thus, however, as sometimes they make " big winners;" but on the average they become hardened to the " call for margins," and resign themselves to almost perpetual losses.

Sooner or later many of them become so reduced by ill-luck that they can no longer swing stocks in 100 share lots. Then they drift over to the offices of the Consolidated Exchange, where they will continue to speculate in ten share lots until " busted."

Some of the small offices are infested by women. A few try their luck in oil, others confine themselves to stocks.

They are women of good character, aside from the propensity to risk their present and future support on the game of chance.

Not all of them belong in New York and adjacent cities. Many come from the South, the West and California.

The Southern ladies are a kind, good-hearted, lively and vivacious race. Some of the older ones were brought up on plantations with numerous slaves to execute their slightest wish. When their personal chattels were confiscated, and they became impoverished by the results of the war, they roamed off into new fields in search of fortune or adventures. Some of them are traveled ladies of the highest intelligence and far-reaching information, who have been nearly all over the world.

In speculation, as a rule, they are too impulsive and quick to jump at wrong conclusions. If they see prices go up a point or two they buy, thinking a big rise is coming sure. But four times out or six they find they have bought at the top and got left. Hence, they seem to suffer worse than the men who are more calculating, cautious and wary.

They are just as rip-roaring bulls, or as rampant

bears as the men. If prices are on the decline they go short on general principles, too often to find they have sold near the bottom and got left again. But no matter, like all votaries of fortune they seldom give up the game as long as they can raise a margin.

One lady was asked if she expected to get rich. She answered, "No! I only want to get even." The cat was out. She had once had money enough to swing stocks by the hundreds of shares. Here she was dealing in ten share lots in hopes of getting back the money she had lost. Fallacious hope!

Another lady who was very unlucky was asked, "Why don't you quit?" She said, "She must get away from family troubles and have some divertisement."

All hands in the market are keen after points. None are more so than the women. "Big men," whom rumor says are operating in this or that stock, are besieged for pointers.

A good story is told at the expense of the late Mr. Woerishoffer. A certain lady was in the habit of looking to him for straight points. One day he spied the lady coming in his office, and not wishing to deceive her, or give his movements away, he hid behind a door. The lady not finding him in took a seat and kept it so long, that Woerishoffer was almost petered out with *ennui* before she got up and left.

Some ladies come in the street in silks, satins, gold jewelry and diamonds. Others show very plain how the fickle jade has treated them, by their well-worn semi-genteel costumes.

A young broker, whose customers were mostly ladies, was asked why they were more unfortunate than the men. Said he :

"Why, blank 'em! The blank-blanked fools always buy at the top, as if prices would never stop going up. They get left and hold on until prices are near the bottom, then they get frightened, sell out and go short as if prices would never stop going down. That's the way they are cleaned out."

CHAPTER XVIII.

THE PETROLEUM EXCHANGE.

THE Consolidated Stock, Mining and Petroleum Exchange is on Broadway, just north of Exchange Place. It extends through to New Street, with the New York Stock Exchange only a few doors above on the opposite side.

This institution is the New York market of the Standard Oil Company's products, and is connected by wire with the Exchange at Oil City.

As long as the concern confined its business to oil and mining stocks "everything was lovely and the goose hung high" between it and the Stock Exchange. Many of the stock brokers became members of the Oil Exchange to carry on deals in that article for their customers.

But when the Consolidated institution began to usurp the functions of the other in dealing in railway stocks and bonds, it gave rise to jealousy and a bitter feeling towards it on the part of the brokers in the old establishment.

So intense did this feeling become, that by order of the Governing Committee of the Stock Exchange, all brokers who had memberships in the Consolidated were compelled to withdraw under penalty of losing their seats in the Stock Exchange, which were worth about $25,000 each.

The Consolidated was dependent on the other Exchange for its quotations of stocks and bonds. Could the brokers of the latter have had their way, it would have been deprived of a connecting ticker service. But it had a contract with the Gold and Stock Telegraph Co., which did not expire until the Spring of 1886.

The Oil Exchange first began dealing in railway stocks and bonds in 1884. Speculators can buy or sell there by the hundred shares, or in fractional lots of ten shares upwards. Stocks could and can be bought in less amounts than 100 shares at the old Exchange, but stock is not easily borrowed to make deliveries on fractional short sales of less than 100 shares. This difficulty is obviated at the Oil Exchange, and small lots can be bought, sold or borrowed freely.

A new ticker service, invented especially for it, came into use in 1886. Now, while the Consolidated Exchange claims to be independent and to make its own quotations, it continues to follow closely the prices made at the Stock Exchange, which latter used to stigmatize its rival, in derision, as nothing but a huge bucket shop.

A large part of the members are young men, many of them " cheap Johns," ravenous for customers and commissions ; who will buy or sell ten share lots for their clients on the smallest margins of 3, 2 and even 1 per cent. They will do the best they can for their customers. But as self-preservation is nature's first law, they will look out for their own safety, first, last, and all the time.

Most all the business is on margins, and a small capital goes a good ways, when they can get the stocks bought for customers, carried on interest by a trust company, which holds the stock bought as collateral.

A young man who can buy a seat costing a few hundred dollars becomes a broker. He then wants a partner who can put up some capital. A cheap office is hired, perhaps, up on a fourth or fifth floor. The partner's business is to attend to customers, and look after the book-keeping; while the broker is in the Board to execute orders.

As a firm they may agree, for mutual safety, not to speculate themselves. The great thing is to get straight points. The office man is always on the alert for points to steer customers in and out. He runs down to the offices of the big brokers, has an ear open to curbstone brokers and everybody for hints as to ups or downs. Then back to the office he is very free with his opinions to influence or lead his clients in long or short.

Notwithstanding the agreement for mutual safety, if the office man thinks he has a straight pointer for a movement of several per cent. up or down, he will, not unfrequently, run down to the bucket shops and buy or sell 100 or 200 shares on

a one per cent. margin unknown to his partner,
the broker. He may win at one time and lose at
another. The infatuation of gambling is on him ;
the stability of the firm rests on a volcano, which
when it bursts will land both of them among the
shorn lambs.

A GIANT MONOPOLY.

The Standard Oil Company is the manipulating
power behind the curtain in all the great movements in petroleum in this country. The time
was when it had practically the entire monopoly
of supplying the markets of the world with this
product. But later, the discovery of immense oil
fields in Russia developed a powerful rival and
brought it into competition with another monopoly in supplying the wants of other nations.

The Nobel Brothers have immense oil works at
Baku, and, it is said, now control more petroleum
than any other concern in the world. Their
wealth is moderately estimated at £80,000,000
sterling.

The uses to which the oil may be adapted are
various, and constantly being increased by new
discoveries. ".The value of the residual product of
petroleum distillation as an efficient and economi-
cal source of steam power is claimed to have been
conclusively established in connection with the
marvelous development by the Brothers Nobel, of
the petroleum industry at the Baku Works, Rus-

-sia, which are fed through pipe lines of an aggregate length of more than sixty miles, by the apparently inexhaustible supplies of the Aspheron Peninsula.

The residual or heavy oil which remains after extracting the illuminating and lubricating oils from the petroleum, and of which the Messrs. Nobel alone now produce 450,000 tons annually, is already used as fuel on upwards of three hundred steamers upon the Caspian Sea and the Volga, and by the locomotives on the Trans-Caucasian and Trans-Caspian railways.

In regard to the employment of refuse petroleum as fuel in locomotive engines, it is claimed that, weight for weight, it has 33 per cent. higher evaporative value than anthracite, and that while 60 per cent. of efficiency is realized with the latter, 75 per cent. is obtained with petroleum refuse."

A CLERK'S BONANZA.

The "pipe line" system, of conveying the oleaginous fluid from the oil regions to the seaboard through conduits, originated with a poor clerk in a New York office. He was in bad health, and his employers sent him to Oil City to fix some business for them, as well as to give him a chance to recuperate.

The shipment of the crude product from the interior to the refineries near tide water in barrels and oil cars was expensive and troublesome.

The clerk fixed his business, then looking around at his leisure, took in the situation, and at last "caught on" to an idea of a series of tanks at distant points with pipes through which the oil could be forced by pumps from one station to another. He kept his own counsel, developed his idea and took out letters patent. There was "millions in it," but he did not know it.

Oil capitalists soon saw the immense value of the invention and offered him $500,000 cash for all his right, title and interest in it.

He was only a poor clerk, on a salary. The sum seemed so enormous he grabbed for it, without a second thought, and sold out. It is said had he retained the whole monopoly of the fruit of his brain, it would have been worth to him $500,000,000.

The manner in which these pipe lines are cleaned, from time to time, is thus described by the New York *Sun :*

The pipes by which petroleum is transported from the oil regions to the seaboard are cleaned by means of a stem $2\frac{1}{2}$ feet long, having at its front end a diaphragm made of wings which can fold on each other, and thus enable it to pass an obstruction it cannot remove. This machine carries a set of steel scrapers somewhat like those used in cleaning boilers. It is put into the pipes and propelled by the pressure transmitted from the pumps from one station to another. Relays of men follow the scraper by the noise it makes in its progress, one party taking up the pursuit as the other is exhausted. They must not let it out of their hear. ing, for if it stops unnoticed its location can only be established by cutting the pipe.

On 10 per cent. margin $1,000 will buy or sell 10,000 barrels of oil, which is equal to 100 shares of stock, and the commissions are the same, $\frac{1}{8}$ each way. The oil is supposed to be on storage, and those who go long of it have to pay an average of about 70 cents a day storage charges on each 10,000 barrels. If oil is cornered, those short of it have to pay loaning rates for borrowed oil to make their deliveries. Oil in tanks is dealt in by pipe line certificates.

CHAPTER XIX.

THE PRODUCE EXCHANGE.

ABOUT forty years ago a few old-time merchants used to meet under an awning on the sidewalk at Broad and South Streets, where they made purchases and sales of grain and produce for home consumption and export from canal boats and coasting vessels, bringing wheat and other truck to New York for a market.

As the business grew and the membership increased, a building was hired, which became known as the Corn Exchange. Here business was done in the actual purchase, sale and delivery of products, free from much of the purely margin-gambling deals with which the bona fide transactions of the present day are mixed.

In 1860 the members had increased to about 700, and increased accommodations were wanted. They raised a fund by subscription among themselves, and purchased the 'block of ground at Whitehall, Water and Pearl Streets. Here they erected the first Produce Exchange building, which was completed in 1861.

In 1879 the membership had increased to over 2,500, and again more room was wanted.

At first, when the Association did business at Broad and South Streets, the initiation fee was $10, which in time was increased to $500, and then to $1,000.

When the scheme of a new and enlarged Exchange was brought up in 1879 the Association had a surplus fund of about $350,000. It was decided to use this money towards the purchase of a new site. Accordingly all that part of the block at the foot of Broadway and along Whitehall Street, extending 307½ feet from Beaver to Stone Street, and running back 150 feet on Beaver and 149 feet on Stone Street, was purchased for $670,000.

In 1882 the corner-stone of the New Produce Exchange was laid, and the structure was completed in 1884. To sustain the enormous weight of the building, about 16,000 piles were used under the foundation, driven down by pile-drivers from fifteen to twenty feet below the cellar.

The New Produce Exchange is one of the largest and most solidly constructed buildings in the city. It is of the Italian renaissance style, modified. The material is of granite to the top of the basement, thence the wall rises in red Philadephia brick and terra cotta to a height of 125 feet above the street.

The portals of the three fronts on Broadway, Beaver and Stone Streets are of white gray granite with engaged columns on the sides of the entrances. The cornices and copings are simple but prominently developed.

On the east end of the building on Stone Street, covering an additional space 40 by 70 feet, is a clock tower in the form of an Italian Campanile, 200 feet high. North of this is a terrace from which is a fourth entrance to the east side of the building.

In the interior, on the first floor, is a magnificent hall about 15 feet wide running through the centre from Stone to Beaver Street, with a transverse hall opening on Broadway, and another hall on the south side opening out on the terrace and clock tower. These halls are tiled with variegated stone in blocks and figures like oil cloth.

The Exchange board room occupies about two-thirds of the upper floors. It is 215 feet long, 134 wide and 60 feet high, lighted by both windows and skylights. On the north end it has a visitors' gallery running the whole width of the room.

On the several floors in the other part of the building are about 300 offices, executive offices, library and coat rooms. All these floors were so designed that the partitions can be taken down and the entire space added to the present arena of the bulls and bears, making one grand room extending the entire length and width of the building.

There are five elevators on the north end and

four on the south end, one of which runs to the roof of the clock tower.

The basement under the south half of the building is used for the vaults of the Produce Exchange Safe Deposit and Storage Company. These vaults occupy a space 125 feet square and contain hundreds of safes for the use of the public, besides plenty of room for the storage of all kinds of valuables. The whole building is fire-proof, and the vaults are claimed to be the strongest burglar proofs in the world.

That the Produce Exchange is a source of great public benefit, in moving the crops and finding a market for our products at home and abroad, cannot be denied. It is equally true that it long since became the scene of immense gambling operations on margins for catchpenny profits in grain and provisions. The same kind of trickery, manipulation, squeezes and corners to put up the price of wheat, corn, pork and lard are resorted to here, and in Chicago, as at the Stock Exchange to put up the price of stocks for a gambling profit. Prices are raided down and remunerative values destroyed for another gambling profit, by many who never become the *bona fide* owners of the stuff, except as it is bought, sold, delivered and really owned by the brokers who carry it for customers on margins. In effect, a large class of customers operate on mere bets, on which profits or losses accrue the same as in any other species of gambling. Certainly the prosperity of the country is not promoted by the operations of the bears to enrich themselves at the expense of the destruction of the values of other people's property.

Aside from these gambling operations, the true legitimate business of the Exchange is of immense benefit to agriculture and commerce.

We have a magnificent country, with agricultural resources scarcely more than half developed. In times past we practically had the monopoly of supplying Europe with grain and many other articles of commerce. We could continue to feed our own fast increasing population and have surplus enough to supply the demands of Europe for generations to come.

The *Produce Exchange Weekly* says :

The acreage of land adapted to wheat culture in the States and Territories of the Pacific coast is estimated at 100,000,000 acres, of which 25,000,000 lie within California, 18,000,000 in Oregon, 10,000,000 in Colorado, 10,000,000 in Idaho, while the area allotted to Montana, Utah and Wyoming is placed at 7,000,000 acres each. The bulk of all this wheat land yet lies untouched, the area of wheat harvested in these States and Territories in 1885 being as follows : California, 2,822,400 acres ; Oregon, 876,102 acres ; Colorado, 120,943 acres ; Idaho, 62,370 acres ; Montana, 83,864 acres ; Utah, 96,861 acres, and Wyoming, 3,180 acres.

And yet, notwithstanding our almost unlimited capacity to supply the shortage of European crops, we are fast losing ground in our exports of bread-stuffs.

In the crop year 1880-1 there were 7,945,786 barrels of flour exported; the year 1883-4 shows 9,152,260 barrels sent abroad, an increase of the value of flour exported for these years of $6,092,439. To make comparisons: for the same years there was a decrease of 80,216,465 bushels of wheat exported, of a decreased money value of $92,671,807.

For the same time in corn there was a decrease of 46,660,665 bushels, of a decreased value of $23,054,570, to our export trade. And a falling off, in the article of pork, of $3,509,570 in value, owing largely to the fear of trichinæ in American pork, started by Chancellor Bismarck, in forbidding its importation into the German Empire.

With the richest wheat lands on the globe, why is it we are falling behind in competing with other parts of the world in export of wheat and flour?

The question is easily answered and is attributable to several causes :

1st. The cost of labor and the enhanced cost of living is, with us, out of all proportion to that of many other countries.

2d. Formerly Russian agriculture, under the Boyards, but little more than sufficed for the wants of its own people. With the abolition of serfdom came a new era. Those who had been slaves of the soil became independent, and had a stimulus to advance their own fortunes. Agriculture began to flourish as it never had before. Russian wheat became a staple article of export.

3d. The opening of the Suez Canal was a prominent factor in the development of Indian commerce, particularly in the culture of wheat for exportation. Labor in India is very cheap; in fact it is cents a day where it is shillings with us, with board thrown in. The short cut by canal across the Isthmus, instead of by the long dangerous circuit around the African Continent, enables India to lay her product down in European markets much cheaper than we can.

Our wheat is much superior, especially the hard red winter wheat of Minnesota and Dakota, to the soft article of India. If the wages of labor and cost of living were equal, we need not fear competition. But the Russian peasant can live at much less cost than can our agricultural laborers, while the wages, including cost of living, to the Indian tiller of the soil represent but a few cents a day. So it is that in the profitable export of this staple we are at a disadvantage.

The *Indian Agricultural Gazette*, published at Calcutta, gives an interesting account of the primitive methods of agriculture employed in India: For wheat the soil is cultivated nine or more times during the rainy season with an implement called a bulthur, a small and light grubber, the working parts of which are two wooden pegs, which go into the ground and are connected by an iron knife, which runs through the soil nine inches deep. This instrument is drawn by a pair of oxen. The seed is sown in November with the use of a deeply penetrating drill, known as the tifan, which has three pegs shod with iron and a hollow bamboo attached to each. The three bamboos converge to a hopper in which the seed grain is placed. This drill penetrates to the depth of about nine inches, and six bullocks are required to draw it. Only 20 lbs. (one-third of a bushel) of wheat per acre are sown, which is about one-fifth of the quantity sown in America, England, etc. The product is usually about 450 lbs., or $7\frac{1}{2}$ bushels per acre. The crop takes three and a half months to mature, and is usually cut with a sickle, but occasionally is pulled out by the roots, after which the grain is trodden out by bullocks. This primitive method of threshing is a serious drawback to Indian wheat, which contains a great deal of dirt in consequence. It is estimated that at least 30,000 tons of dirt and foreign matter were transported with last year's crop, entailing great expense, not only in the way of freight charges, but in the removal of the objectionable materials by special washing and cleaning process in milling.

CHAPTER XX.

THE COTTON EXCHANCE.

THE first attempt to organize a Cotton Exchange in New York was made in 1868. It took shape in the formation of the New York Board of Cotton Brokers, and in 1870 became known as the Cotton Exchange.

It began with 100 names, and has grown to a membership of about 500. With the new organization in 1870, many changes in the method of transacting business were introduced. Dealings in futures began to form an important part of the business. This feature at first excited a strong prejudice; but it has been increasing in favor with the cotton men ever since. Like all the other Exchanges, a great deal of its true legitimate business is mixed up with pure speculative gambling—a bulling up of prices for one profit and a bearing down for another.

The new Cotton Exchange building is an imposing edifice, situated on Beaver Street, in the immediate locality of the Custom House. It cost, with the ground on which it stands, over $1,000,000. The dimensions of the building are

87½ feet on Beaver Street, 116 feet on William Street, and 89 feet on Pearl Street.

It is in the French renaissance style. The basement and part of the first story is built of oolitic limestone. Above it is of buff brick and terra cotta, with a red slate roof.

From the curb to the main roof the height is 130 feet ; to the top of the tower it is 156 feet, and the flag-staff brings up the height to 200 feet. In the main story is the Exchange Hall, or board room, which is 108 feet long, 70 feet wide, with the ceiling 35 feet high. The floors of the six office stories are of encaustic tiles. There are about 900 tons of ironwork ; the heaviest cast iron columns weigh about 7,300 pounds each, and are 28 inches in diameter, and 2 inches thick ; these are connected by wrought iron girders, weighing 2½ tons, on which the iron floor beams rest. The roof and towers are framed of iron, and an iron framework suspended from the beams above sustains the plastered ceiling of the main room.

CHAPTER XXI.

PUBLIC STOCK EXCHANGES.

BUCKET SHOPS, as they are called in derision by the regular brokers, are very numerous.
The number in New York city is estimated at
fifty. Many of these have branches in various
cities and large villages in other parts of the
country.

There are clusters of them on lower Broadway
and New Street. Others are on Broad and Beaver
Streets. Some are in the locality of the City Hall
and scattered here and there in different parts of
the city. One double building, running through
from Broadway to New Street, had six of them,
all with a large class of customers.

Some deal in stocks only; others in stocks,
oil, corn, wheat, pork, lard and cotton futures.

No stock, oil, grain, or provisions are actually
bought or sold, except in case of necessity. The
contracts are in the nature of put and call privileges, and in rare instances a literal performance
and actual delivery can be required. Invariably
the deal is a pure gamble on the turn of the market. Customers want profits. The shops want

profits. Neither want the article called for by the contracts.

These places are eyesores to the regular Exchange men. They are jealous of any competition which draws away custom and cuts into their commission profit account. That this jealousy is well founded can readily be seen, when it is alleged that the aggregate business of the bucket shops is often larger than that of the Stock Exchange.

The bucket shops were long since deprived of direct quotations from the Stock Exchange over the Gold and Stock, and the Commercial Company's indicators. But they get their quotations all the same, in an indirect way, by private wires and telephones from unsuspected allies.

One shop was said to get its quotations by the roundabout way of Poughkeepsie. Some have five or six telephones, in a row, on the walls of their private office, so that if information fails in one direction they can get it instantly from another. The Exchange brokers growl and threaten, but are powerless. They are a unit in favor of legislation to close the bucket shops, but when it comes to legal interference with their own practices, they harp on another string.

In the Winter of 1886–7 Senator Vedder introduced a bill in the New York Legislature, proposing to levy a tax of one-fiftieth of 1 per cent. on speculative transactions in stocks, bonds, wheat,

cotton and other articles.   This in effect was a tax
on all purchases or sales on margins which make
up the bulk of the business done at the Exchanges, and practically all of that done at the
bucket shops.

A committee of the Senate took testimony in
New York as to the effect of such a tax.   Stock
and Produce Exchange men fought it tooth and
nail, denouncing it as " a tax on commerce and a
boycott on their business ;" and a threat that if
such a bill became a law, it would cause the removal of the Exchanges out of the State to Jersey
City.   They said : " If you want to do away with
the bucket shops make laws to that effect."

Now, in a moral point of view there is no difference whether one gambles on 1 per cent. margins and upwards at the bucket shops, or on 5 or
10 per cent. margins at the Exchanges. The effect
is just as demoralizing in one as in the other.

The only difference is the brokers will buy, own
and carry, or sell short and carry stock on customers' orders, for fat commissions, if they are protected by sufficient margin against loss.   On the
other hand the customers, other than investors,
never intend to pay for and possess the stock they
order bought, or they do not own and cannot deliver the stock they order sold short. They simply
play a game of chance on the turn of the market,
just as the man who puts down a sum of money

on a card or faro board plays a game of chance on the turn of the pack.

Between the bucket shops and their customers it is a game of chance, pure and simple, with no pretense of handling any stock at all. And this game of chance turns on the game played at the Stock Exchange itself, or on the deals in oil, grain, provisions and cotton.

Comparing the evils of gambling in the Stock Exchange banking and brokerage offices with that of the bucket shops, the latter are by far the less harmful and costly. If a man is bound to speculate and begins small in these shops, his chances for profits are just as good, and he can get his eye teeth cut at far less expense than under the influences in the banker-broker offices, where he will, only too often, be roped in and out of ventures and milked for fat commissions.

In the other places the game is between the shops and their customers : the interests of one side are antagonistic to that of the other. For the shop men, to bring influences to bear to induct customers into this or that, would be useless and only arouse suspicion.

At the Stock Exchange the real trouble is that the business is run in the interest of the brokers and the big manipulators, and not of the public at their back. Interest is charged at 6 per cent. even when stocks can be carried at 2 per cent. Shaves are demanded of the short interest and not always credited to those long of the stocks lent, unless the customers keep a sharp lookout and question their brokers, when they see by the news tissues that a loaning rate is imposed. And commissions are ¼ per cent. on a turn in each 100 shares.

In the bucket shops there is no interest to pay and no loaning rates. The commissions are only one-eighth per cent., except on deals closed out the same day as made, when it is one-eighth each way.

To illustrate how much more dangerous margin gambling is in a broker's office than in a bucket shop :

Suppose a man buys 100 shares of Lackawanna at $135 a share on a margin of $1,000. 100 shares at 135 is $13,500. Now, if the price should go below 135 and he holds on for sixty days and his margin is not wiped out, he would be charged interest on cost and be credited with interest on his margin, making a difference against him of $125, besides the loss he stood for on the stock and the commissions. If the deal was closed in 60 days by the loss of his margin, he would be out of pocket $1,000 on margin, $125 on interest, and $25 on commissions. Total loss, $1,150.

If he was a bear and sold the same thing short on the same margin, if the market went against him, and he held on and the stock was squeezed with a loaning rate of ⅛ or $12.50 one day ; 1 per cent. or $100 the next day, and 4 per cent. or $400 the third day, his loss with his margin wiped out would be $1,000 on margin ; $512.50 on loaning rates, and $25 on commissions. Total loss, $1,537.50.

However, if the customer was unable to put up more margin, or make good any deficit, the broker would, for his own protection, close him out before the margin was exhausted. This the broker is not always able to do, for events happen like a stroke of lightning. In such a case, the broker would harry his customer with a law suit and a judgment for the deficit, and perhaps place him on the jail limits for debt.

In the bucket shops the usual way is to put up 1 per cent. margin, and to this additional margins can be added any time before the margins that are on are exhausted. Hence a man can take the chances on 100 full shares of Lack. by putting up 1 per cent. If the price declines one point before he has put on more margin, his contract is wiped out and he loses $100, but no more. If he has made his margin 2 per cent. and the price declines to that extent with no more margin put on, he loses $200. If the whole market is weak and declining he will generally drop out of the deal with this loss. If he was a bear and went short with the market against him, the same losses would result in a reverse ratio. There is no such thing as interest and loaning rates in the bucket shops to add to his losses.   The commissions are included in the margins he lost.

The business is conducted fair, square and above board.   The quotations are the prices made at the New York Stock Exchange, and are announced by the caller and posted on the boards by the marker, without any appreciable loss of time.

The manipulation, trickery and rumors to lead or mislead, all originate from those who operate at the big machine.   These things have the same influence with the customers at the bucket shops as with the other class of speculators at the brokers' offices.   The shops have nothing to do with trickery, manipulation and the rumor mill.   That is all done for them to perfection.

The bucket shops are generally large rooms, with a space partitioned off for the telegraph operators, caller, book-keepers and cashier, the dividing partition being about five feet high.   The boards on which the quotations are posted on large print cards, are opposite or on one side within full view of the caller and clerks.

The first parallel column on the boards gives the closing quotations of the day before.

Next under are the abbreviated designations of the various stocks dealt in, and the quotations are carried down from them in horizontal columns. See table illustrated.

135½	95⅞	115⅜	113⅝	102	92⅜	75⅝	68¾	62⅛	34¼	38⅛	32⅝	58⅝	28	63¾
D. L.	L. S.	N.W.	N.Y.C.	D. H.	St. P.	W. U.	J. C.	L. N.	Erie.	R'd'g.	O. T.	U. P.	N. P.	Oil.
135½	95¾	115¼	113⅝	102⅛	92⅜	75⅝	68⅝	62	34¼	38	32⅝	58¾	28	63⅞
135⅜	95⅞	115⅛	113½	102	92¼	75¾	68½	61⅞	34⅛	38⅛	....	58⅞	28⅛	64
135¼	95¾	115	......	101⅞	92⅜	75⅞	68⅝	61⅞	....	38	....	58¾	28	64⅛
135⅜	95⅝	......	......	....	92¼	....	68½	....	....	37⅞	....	58⅝	...	64
135⅛	95⅛	......	......	....	92⅛	....	68⅜	....	....	37¾	....	58½	...	63⅞
135	....	......	......	....	92¼	....	68¼	....	....	37⅝	....	....	...	63¾
134⅞	....	......	......	....	....	....	68⅜	....	....	37¾	....	....	...	63⅝
134¾	....	......	......	....	....	....	68½	....	....	37⅝	....	....	...	...
134⅞	....	......	......	....	....	....	....	....	....	37½	....	....	...	...
134¾	....	......	......	....	....	....	....	....	....	37⅝	....	....	...	...
......	....	......	......	....	....	....	....	....	....	37½	....	....	...	...
......	....	......	......	....	....	....	....	....	....	37⅝	....	....	...	...
......	....	......	......	....	....	....	....	....	....	37¾	....	....	...	...
......	....	......	......	....	....	....	....	....	....	38	....	....	...	...
......	....	......	......	....	....	....	....	....	....	38⅛	....	....	...	...
......	....	......	......	....	....	....	....	....	....	38¼	....	....	...	...
......	....	......	......	....	....	....	....	....	....	38⅛	....	....	...	...

If there are any underhand dealings, it may be the managers find on inspecting their books, after the close of the day's business, that they have say 15,000 shares out at the main and branch offices, with the customers on the right side against them. In such a case what is to hinder the bucket shops from buying or selling 3,000 or 4,000 shares at the Stock Exchange with a view of turning the market in a contrary direction to wipe out the profits, if not the margins, on the 15,000 shares held against them ? If the trick succeeds, of course they can skin their customers and close out the 3,000 or 4,000 shares at the Stock Exchange at a good profit besides.

All the bucket shops make contracts on 1 per cent. margins and upwards. In some the margins and profits are unlimited. In others the liabilities are limited to 5 per cent., to 3 per cent., and sometimes to 1 per cent. on certain very erratic stocks. Sometimes also the margin put up is limited to 5 per cent.

The chances of guessing the market are the same here as at the Stock Exchange. As a rule customers guess wrong from three times out of five to four times out of six in the long run. The bucket men know this and calculate on it, that the margin of profit in the long run is largely in their favor.

Still the business is not always profitable. The

bull market in 1885 ran so long one way, it was like bucking against fate to go short of it. The margins of those who took the bear side as prices advanced, were wiped out to the immense profit of the shops. When the crowd turned and caught on right it was like picking up money in the street. Almost every venture brought profits, and the bucket shops suffered terribly, some of them being compelled to bust.

The exhaustion of the boom left the crowd thoroughly imbued with bull sentiments, and as long as they continued to operate on that side their margins were wiped into the money drawers of the bucket men at a great rate.

One shop issued dodgers, offering to take risks on from 5 to 5,000 shares of stock, and on from 500 to 500,000 bushels of grain at a single quotation, and correspondingly on pork and lard.

No grain or provisions are ever handled, or intended to be. If any are seen, it must be the crackers, cheese, bologna, and an inch square piece of pork, in the centre of a pan of baked beans, on the free lunch sideboard, in the basement saloon down below.

Some shops which combine stocks and oil with deals in grain and provisions, have a posted scale for margins on deals based on Chicago quotations for corn, wheat, pork and lard, viz :

Margin on grain at one cent per bushel.

$5 buys or sells.........500 bushels.

10   "   "   " ....1,000.   "

100 "   "   " 10,000   "

1,000 ·· "   " 100,000   "

On pork at 25 cents per barrel.

$6.25 buys or sells...........25 bbls.

12.50 "   "   " ....50 "

25.00 "   "   " ....100 "

250.00 "   "   " ....1,000 "

2,500.00 "   "   " ....10,000 "

On lard at 48 cents per tierce.

$12 buys or sells...........25 tierces.

24   "   "   " ....50 "

48   "   "   " ....100 "

480 "   "   " ....1,000 "

4,800 "   "   " ....10,000 "

On stocks at one per cent.

$10 buys or sells........... 10 shares.

100 "   "   ·· ....100 "

1,000 "   "   " ....1,000 "

Some shops limit the number of shares to 100 or 200 on a single deal. But few will make contracts on over 1,000 shares at one quotation. The lowest limit is 5 shares in all of them.

Orders must be handed in, and contracts closed out when the figures are fresh on the boards. One class of stocks may be active and advance or decline one or two points, when the prices of another class remain stationary. To expect the shops to make contracts based on old quotations, which are one or two per cent. below the movements of the rest of the market, would be unjust; for these stocks which have not moved will often spurt up or down a half or a full point at a single jump to catch up to the others. One class of stocks carry the others up or down with them in sympathy.

Customers make their own selections of stock and price as the quotations appear.

Orders with a margin are handed in, which, if prices agree with those fresh on the boards, are accepted and contracts made. These the customer can close out, at his will, to catch a profit, or to stop a loss, any time before the margin is exhausted, from the last figures fresh on the boards. Settlements are made promptly. The contracts have ninety days to run.

Copies of contracts are similar to the following, with variations :

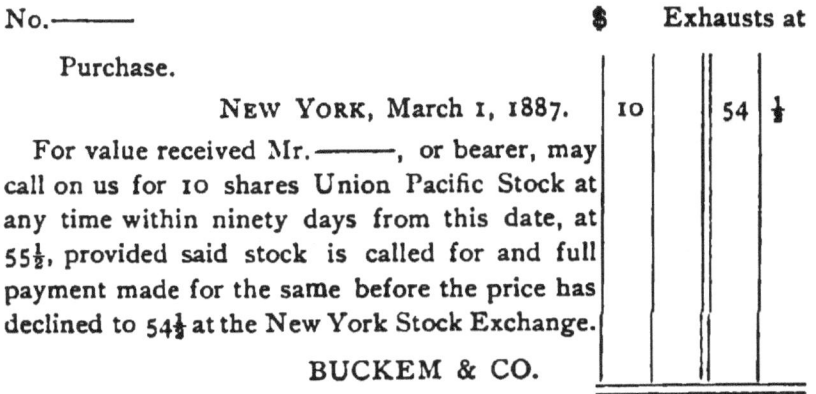

No.—— $ Exhausts at

Purchase.

NEW YORK, March 1, 1887.   10   54 $\frac{1}{4}$

For value received Mr.——, or bearer, may call on us for 10 shares Union Pacific Stock at any time within ninety days from this date, at 55$\frac{1}{2}$, provided said stock is called for and full payment made for the same before the price has declined to 54$\frac{1}{4}$ at the New York Stock Exchange.

BUCKEM & CO.

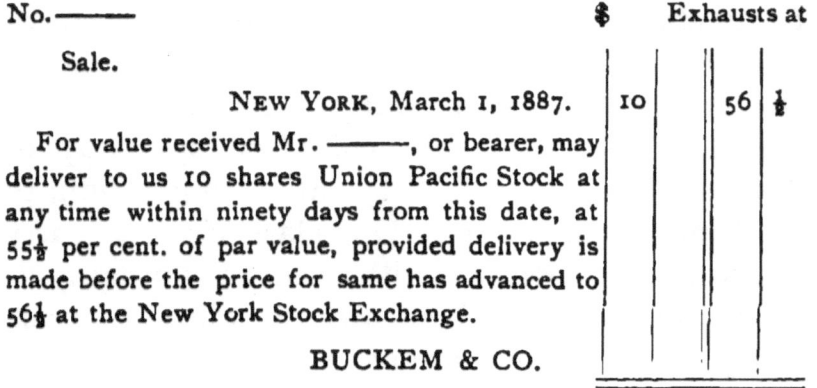

No.——— $ Exhausts at

    Sale.

         NEW YORK, March 1, 1887.   10   56 ¼

    For value received Mr.———, or bearer, may deliver to us 10 shares Union Pacific Stock at any time within ninety days from this date, at 55½ per cent. of par value, provided delivery is made before the price for same has advanced to 56¼ at the New York Stock Exchange.

            BUCKEM & CO.

Additional margins, if put on, are carried down in the cash column, and the exhaust limit is extended in proportion.

People do not lose money as fast in these places, as those who speculate through brokers at the Stock Exchange. The reason is the brokers usually want $1,000 margin for their own protection, then if the market goes against their customers their advice always is to "hold on." They hold on too long, until the larger part of the margin is exhausted, and then throw over their stock. To do a decent business they must handle at least 100 shares of stock at a time, or they are of no account.

Interest, loaning rates and double commissions are exacted. What wonder then that people flock down to the bucket shops, where the chances of speculation are just as good, the cost nothing but a one-eighth commission and the risk only the one per cent. or two per cent. margin they put up?

The big manipulators of the stock market can make up pools of one hundred or two hundred millions of dollars. They have the power to boom up prices, figuratively, as high as Gilderoy's kite. But unless they can draw in an army of small purse people to buy their stuff, they cannot get out again with the profits they are after.

The withdrawal of so many small operators from the brokers' offices to the bucket shops often works to foil the conspiracies of the great Moguls of "the Street," whose plan was to leave every fool in the lurch in the final culmination of their schemes.

There are times when the bucket shops of New York probably do four times the business done in the main temple of Mammon. The brokers growl and threaten retaliatory measures of all sorts, at which the bucket men, metaphorically, only put their thumbs to their noses and wiggle their fingers.

The business is a lucrative and profitable one to the brokers. But it is an immensely losing one to the general run of their customers.

The business is a losing one to the players at the bucket shops, else how could these places thrive and pay high rents, gas, electric light and telegraph bills, and furnish a living to the proprietors and a squad of clerks ?

As to legislative action to close these places : in the Winter of 1885–6 Assemblyman Cantor in-

troduced a bill to close the bucket shops. Those
interested only laughed and predicted it could not
be done. And nothing was done.

They argued that if such a bill were to become
a law, it would close out all dealings in privileges
dealt in by the big men of the stock market.

The reader will observe that the bucket shop
contracts are in the nature of privileges, in which
stock may be "called for" from, or "delivered
to" the makers of the contract. Now any customer may tender full pay for, and demand the
stock specified in his "Purchase" contract, or
he may have stock which he can put to the maker
of his "Sale" contract and demand the full price
as stated therein. In such a case the makers
could be compelled to a literal performance. This,
however, is not required. All the customers want
is their profits which they get.

Just such a case as this happened in 1886. A
certain stock was very erratic, with wide fluctuations. One man took contracts, on the bull side,
on 1,000 shares of it. The market went his way,
and one day he saw a profit of $10,087.50 in sight.
He handed in his contracts to be closed out; but
the bucket man demurred that the sum was too
large, and offered him, as alleged, $3,000 to settle.
This he would not accept. He then took counsel,
obtained about $70,000, and with this, as alleged,
he tendered full payment, and demanded the stock,
which was refused. Suit was then brought, and

an Examiner was appointed by a Justice of the Supreme Court to take testimony. The result was the bucket men raised their offer to $5,000 to settle, and in the end the whole thing was compromised for $8,000, without a trial, if the reports in the papers are to be relied on.

The bucket shops are very careful to keep so near the legal line that any legislation against them will embrace the Stock Exchange brokers as well. Some of them give notice on their printed orders and contracts that they " solicit and will receive no business except with the understanding that the *actual delivery* of property bought or sold upon orders is in all cases contemplated and understood."

However well the thing may be understood, all that continues to be wanted is the profits, without the delivery of the article specified.

There are rich speculators in the bucket shops as well as the wrecks of the Street who come there from the brokers' offices.

BUCKET SHOP MORALITY.

The following are some of the arguments and specious sophistry used by bucket shop men in defense of their business. The same arguments and line of reasoning apply with the brokers when they offer excuses for their share of the business. Says the bucket man :

" Always bear in mind that 'points' are worthless, and that all speculation is 'guesswork.' The
least informed individual is just as liable to prove
a profitable 'guesser' as the most experienced
Wall Street speculator."

" A great many good and pious people declare
that the stock speculator is a mere gambler, and
hence stock speculation must be avoided by all
reputable people."

" This criticism is born of antiquated dry rot.
It may have been orthodox among the Puritans
when they hovered about Plymouth Rock, but the
country has outgrown the blue laws period."

" It is just as lawful to buy stocks when a limited
demand makes them cheap, and sell them when an
active demand causes them to rise, as it is to buy
or sell any product of nature."

" Stock speculation presents the best avenue yet
discovered for the exercise of the irrepressible activity of the American character. To stigmatize
it as gambling, in the ordinary sense of the term,
is nonsensical and slanderous."

" It is tremendously attractive to the sharp,
aspiring Yankee, who is boiling over with a desire
to get rich quick, because he sees a chance to get
larger sums on a smaller risk, in quicker time than
in any other way."

" He knows that it is largely a matter of chance,
and that it does not in any way interfere with his

being a moral man and a good citizen, therefore he embarks in it."

"Stocks and securities represent the property of the corporations which issue them, each certificate being entitled to its pro rata share of the same, and there is no legal or moral reason why they should not be purchased and sold in the market precisely the same as any merchantable commodity."

"Merchants buy a hundred barrels of pork or lard for purposes of trade and profit. They hold these for an advance, and generally sell when it comes. Men buy a hundred shares of stock on the same principle, and sell for the same reason. They engage in trade to make money. They buy and sell stocks to make money. It is a struggle to get rich in both cases, and philanthropy plays no figure in the race."

"As long as men stand a chance, by trading in stocks, to make from 500 to 1,000 per cent. more money in one-fiftieth of the time, and with one-fiftieth of the risk (sic?) than they can realize by trading in merchandise, they will select stocks in preference. This is the Alpha and Omega of the whole business."

THE REALITY.

The subtle reasoning and fallacious arguments in the foregoing are very eloquent, plausible, and fine in theory. The arch enemy of mankind once, upon a time at least, was just as eloquent, plausible and theoretical.

In point of fact, the investor who buys stocks and bonds ; the merchant who buys grain, pork, lard, or any other species of merchandise and has it delivered to him, becomes the absolute owner of real tangible property. These men who own and hold stocks, bonds, grain, pork, etc., for an advance make an honest profit by selling when it comes, and give an honest value in the delivery of actual property.

There is, and can be, no analogy between the men who own real tangible property and make an honest profit out of it, and the men who put up margin to make a gambling profit out of wind they do not own, out of atmosphere they cannot grasp, and out of gas they cannot confine.

It is right in between these two classes of traders that philanthropy does come in and plays a tremendous moral figure in the race. The bucket shop speculators simply make bets on chances with nothing tangible back of it for delivery. The margin speculators, at the brokers' offices are in the same boat : they make bets on chances, with nothing back of it that they actually own, or intend to own, and can deliver. Besides this they bet on chances to make a profit at the expense and loss of some one else who gets no value.

THE EFFECT.

In effect the whole business of dealing in stocks, oil, grain, provisions and cotton futures on margins, as practiced by the Stock, Produce, Petroleum and Cotton Exchanges and the Bucket Shops, with the attendant trickery, deception and manipulation to allure in and mulct the people by wholesale, is debasing and demoralizing to a far greater degree than any other legal or illegal business on the American Continent.

The votaries of the game of chance become absorbed and enslaved by hallucination in the hazardous business. When they have been cleaned out to the extent that they can no longer swing a hundred share lot at the brokers' offices, they descend down on the bucket shops and continue the game as long as they can put up the lowest limit of margin.

The business brutalizes the mind, and to a more or less extent hardens, if it does not destroy, the finer feelings of the human heart.

The bucket shop men are far more honest and innocent in this: that they do not make or unmake the market, or work the inhuman machinery of allurement and deception. That is all done for them. They honestly present the market as it is made by the superior powers and influences. The contracts are made on the basis of the customer's own guess and selection.

13

There may be one chance that a man can get suddenly rich at the vicarious game. But there are ninety-nine chances that he will not make a big strike and retire with it. He will risk it again and again until it disappears.

CHAPTER XXII.

A LOWER SCALE OF GAMBLING.

IN December, 1886, there was opened in New Street a room, which was an original improvement on the bucket shop method of bucking the tiger. Quotations of stocks actually bought and sold at the markets were done away with. In place of the stock ticker, there was a clock with an annunciator which rings every half minute or so. At every ring figured cards fall from some hidden receptacle inside the clock and the figures on the cards state that D. N. has declined $\frac{1}{2}$, or that T. P. M. has advanced $\frac{1}{4}$, or O. T. has improved $\frac{1}{8}$, etc. A boy marker records this on the boards under the letters indicated.

On one of the walls of the room was a blackboard divided into five panels. At the top of these panels were the letters D. L. B. ; T. P. M. ; J. M. C. ; D. N., and O. T. From these letters the figures which came out on the cards from the clock were carried down the columns.

What these initials represented the crowd in the room did not know. O. T. might mean Oregon Trans-Continental, but it did not, for that stock was quoted at the New York Stock Exchange in

the thirties, and here O. T. was being bought or
sold at 113 to 115. The fact was that the initials
represented fictitious things and stood in the place
of real stocks. If the manager or assistants in the
shop were asked for explanations, they replied
humorously that D. L. B. meant Delaware Lug-
gage Bureau ; T. P. M., Toledo Postmaster, and
so on to the end of the chapter.

Late in the afternoon the blackboards would be
white with figures, and the room crowded. The
record on the boards showed that these fictitious
stocks had fluctuated up and down during the
day within a limit of five points. Nearly everybody had a shabby, hungry look.

Margins did not exceed $5, and were generally
less than half that sum. Quotations were ground
out on time, there was no weary waiting. Money
that was lost or occasionally made, was lost or made
promptly.

The thing was gambling pure and simple. The
figures come out on the principle of a battery,
worked to turn the margin of profits in favor of the
bank, no matter which way the crowd bet. It had
the advantage of not being obliged to close up when
business hours were over, but could keep on running as long as the presence of the crowd made it
profitable. This place was pulled by the police
after a few days.

Later in the Winter another concern, calling itself " The Indicator Stock Exchange," was started

on another street, and purported to have offices at New York, Baltimore and Washington. The quotations seemed to come in by telegraph. The peculiar stocks dealt in were just as mysterious as in the concern first mentioned. The order blanks to buy or sell were under the heading : " We solicit and receive no business, except with the under-standing that the actual delivery of property bought or sold upon orders is in all cases contem-plated and understood." This doubtless was a blind against legal interference.

CHAPTER XXIII.

BIG BUSINESS ON SMALL CAPITAL.

THERE are Stock Exchange brokerage firms with not over $25,000 cash capital. These are considered very weak; $100,000 capital is decent, but not strong; $500,000 capital is strong and respectable, while those houses which can show $1,000,000 and upwards are called A 1, gilt edged.

The following will no doubt be a curious exhibit of how a firm's credit may be stretched and an enormous business done on a very small capital, comparatively. Speculators take terrific risks to make big profits on a turn of the market. Stock houses take enormous risks to extend their business and increase their commission profits.

A firm's own capital is, say.............	$100,000
5 Customers put up margins of $50,000 each	250,000
10 Customers put up margins of $25,000 each	250,000
20 Customers put up margins of $10,000 each	200,000
20 Customers put up margins of $5,000 each	100,000

20 Customers put up margins of $1,000
    each $20,000
———————

The firm has capital and margin in
    hand of......................... $920,000

Speculative stocks may range in price from $140 a share for gilt-edged down to $10 a share for the cats and dogs. Usually there will be more of the medium and low-priced stocks bought for speculation than of the high-priced ones. So, calling the average price $60 a share, a stock firm can use the stocks they have paid for to hypothecate as collateral to the banks for loans of money with which to buy and pay for more stock. This system of hypothecating and buying and rehypothecating for money to buy can be carried to an almost indefinite extent before the credit to borrow money and the ability to buy stock is exhausted. The banks will loan about 80 per cent. of market value on good stock collateral. The following figures will illustrate the process:

Stock firm with capital and margin in
    hand of......................... $920,000
This, at $60 per share, will buy and pay
    for shares....................... 15,300
15,300 shares, at 80 per cent. of value,
    borrows.......................... $734,400
$734,400 pays for shares.............. 12,200
12,200 shares borrows................ $585,600

$585,600 pays for shares................ 9,700
9,700 shares borrows................... $465,600
$465,600 pays for shares................ 7,700
7,700 shares borrows.................. $369,600
$369,600 pays for shares............... 6,100

Here would be 51,000 shares of stock bought and $3,075,200 of stock firms' capital, customers' margins and money borrowed on stock collateral —all on a basis of $100,000 of the firms' own capital; and the last 6,100 shares of stock bought could be hypothecated for $292,800 more money. To carry the thing to the extreme limit of buying and borrowing credit capacity is unnecessary, as the foregoing is sufficient to give an idea of the tremendous risks taken by Wall Street men.

This system of doing a big business on a small capital is a common practice, and is probably often carried beyond the extent here shown. Stocks are bought, paid for and carried on 10 per cent. margins, or even less, by the broker firms for their customers. The firms' margin, or pawn, the stocks they carry to the banks to obtain more money to buy more stock. If the banks lend 80 per cent. of the market value on the stock, it is equivalent to 20 per cent. of margin against the banker-brokers as a protection from loss by a decline in the market. The banks lend their money conditionally that they can call in their loans at any time, or that the brokers must put up more margin to protect

the banks on their loans. If the banker-brokers
fail to return the money when called for, the banks
will throw their stock collateral on the market to
save themselves from loss.

Every bank which loans money on stock collateral has a ticker. The President, Cashier, or
Loan Clerk are supposed to bear in mind the
securities they have and watch the quotations
closely. If danger appears imminent, instant action is taken to protect the bank.

The system of doing a brokerage business, as
illustrated by the foregoing figures, makes the
speculating customers all bulls, and their deals to
remain stationary, while all the stock is being
bought and hypothecated to obtain loans. In
point of fact customers are buying and selling and
taking profits or losses all the time. Both stocks
and money are being turned over .and over again
unless it be that the market is steadily advancing
and all are holding on for big profits.

Then, again, almost every office has its quota of
bears who put up 10 per cent. margin and sell
stock they don't have to sell. All this bear margin is so much surplus capital in the hands of the
banker-broker, and he can use it to help buy stocks
for his bull customers.

The money realized from the sale of stock the
bear did not have. is used as a tender to borrow
stock to keep good the deliveries on short sales
until the bear has covered his shorts. When

stocks loan flat the market value, without premium, is exchanged for the loan of the stock from day to day. If stocks loan at a premium and prices have gone against the bear, all deficits are of course drawn from his margin.

If all the customers of an office are bears, the broker can do an enormous business without a dollar of capital of his own. No money is wanted to buy stock. The money from short stock sold is used to borrow for delivery or to buy stock to close out the deal. The bear margins aggregate a large capital in the hands of the broker for his protection.

CHAPTER XXIV.

OFFICE EXPENSES.

THE expense of running a well-appointed brokerage office is very large. Room is so valuable in the vicinity of the Stock Exchange that the rent is often made so much a square foot. A well located office, twenty-five feet square, will rent for $10,000, which is $16 a square foot. This space is divided off into a reception room, stock room for customers, a private office, and bankers' and brokers' rooms.

The next largest expense is for clerk hire. A managing clerk, say $50 a week. An under clerk, $35 a week. Three other clerks, $30 each per week, and two messengers at $10 a week each. Total, $195 per week. Total per year for clerk hire, $10,140.

Some offices have three or four stock indicators, one oil indicator and one grain and provision ticker, besides news tape and news tissue service. Deals in oil, provisions and cotton are exceptional, however, in a stock office.

The expense of two stock tickers is about $30 a month. News ticker and news tissue service about $15 a month each. Total, $720 a year.

Blank books, stationery, postage, printing and advertising is a heavy item. " Railroad Statistics," or the " Financial Review," given away perhaps to hundreds of customers, is another heavy expense. The Commercial Agency reports of R. G. Dun & Co., and Bradstreet, and the Wall Street publications kept on file, with telephone, telegraph and outside messenger fees, altogether would aggregate about $1,500.

To sum up : rent, $10,000 ; clerk hire, $10,140 ; tickers and news service, $720 : miscellaneous, $1,500, would in round numbers make a grand total expense of at least $22,000 per year. All of which must go in the annual balance sheet before there is any show of a profit.

Other houses doing from five to twenty times as much business have expense accounts of from $30,000 to $50,000 and even more.

Inferior houses get along on $10,000 or even $5,000 a year for expenses. Small one-horse brokers, dealing in ten share lots and upwards at the Consolidated Exchange, can skin along for from $500 to $1,000 expenses a year, in confined quarters, up on the top floor of five and six story buildings.

Notwithstanding the large expenses of first-class houses, some brokerage firms, who never speculate a dollar themselves, grow immensely rich solely out of their commission profits.

No business is more safe·and profitable than commission brokerage, if it is conducted on a non-speculative basis. Conservative houses make sure of safe margins, take their commissions and interest, and leave all the risks to their customers.

EXTENT OF THE BUSINESS.

In a very active market the business done in a day at the New York Stock Exchange is often enormous. During the boom` of 1885´ the sales for many days at a time ran from 500,000 to 800,000 shares per diem.

Houses with a good clientage dealt in from 5,000 to 150,000 shares in five hours of business. On 10,000 shares ⅛ commission is $1,250; on 50,000 shares it is $6,250; on 100,000 shares it is $12,500, and on 150,000 shares it is $18,750 net commissions, if full rates are charged. But more or less of the purchases and sales on the largest transactions of any one house are on the orders of other brokers, at $2 and $4 on each 100 shares, which makes a wide difference. The house that did 150,000 shares in a day, perhaps got full rates on 50,000 shares, and brokers' commission on the balance.

It was estimated that one of the largest operators in the boom of 1885 bought not less than 500,000 shares, and probably a great deal more; and on this he paid full rate commissions of one-eighth each way to buy and sell, making the commissions on the turn of 500,000 shares $125,000, which went to his brokers. He could afford it, for he probably cleared not less than $10,000,000 on his deal in a few months.

In the Fall or Winter, after the recovery from the May panic of 1884, one large operator was known to have sold 250,000 shares of the stock of a single railroad, besides having large holdings of other stocks. He picked up his speculative line around panic prices and made large profits. As he paid full rates the commissions on the turn in 250,000 shares of a single stock were $62,500.

When transactions are very large, it often happens that perhaps one-fourth or more of the total sales are not kept account of from day to day.

In the testimony before the Senate Committee in relation to a tax on speculative transactions, "the Secretary of the Stock Exchange testified that the reported transactions in 1886 were as follows : 103,952,804 shares of listed stocks; $13,367,100 of Government bonds ; $635,937,320 of State and railroad bonds, and 41,000,000 shares of unlisted stocks."

Now to strike an average between the very high and very low price stocks, suppose we lump the entire reported sales of listed and unlisted stocks at $50 a share, the entire cash value would be $7,247,640,200 in stocks alone, exclusive of all other securities. If full rate commissions were exacted on the whole 144,952,804 shares of listed

and unlisted stocks, the commissions would be
$18,119,100.50 to divide up among the 1,100 brok-
ers of the Stock Exchange, which would give each
one $16,471.90, exclusive of commissions on all
other securities. But in fact this is not so, for
many brokers buy or sell for themselves free, or
execute brokers' orders at commissions of $2 and
$4 on each 100 shares. Just where the dividing
line is, in the aggregate transactions between outsiders at full commissions, and brokers at fractional rates, it would be hard to say.

The largest transactions of any one day ever
known at the New York Stock Exchange, were on
December 15, 1886. Almost everybody was long
of stocks. Money on call was manipulated up to
365 per cent. per annum. This caused a great
scare among margin operators who had to pay
interest. They threw their stocks on the market
in wild alarm. The sales for that one day as
reported by the ticker were 1,096,509 shares, but
it was estimated that the total transactions were
full 1,600,000 shares at the Stock Exchange, and
it was said that 500,000 shares more changed
hands at the Consolidated Exchange, making a
grand total of 2,100,000 shares in one day. On
these full rate commissions would be $262,500.
If we were to estimate that day's business done
in all the bucket shops in the city at 1,000,000
shares, and add it to that done at the two Exchanges, the total would be 3,100,000 shares.

And these at $50 a share would represent $155,000,000 in stock deals for one day.

INTEREST PROFITS.

From January, 1884, up to the first few months of 1886 money was so plentiful that call loans could be had from day to day at from 1 to 3 per cent. per annum. Brokerage houses could obtain all the money they wanted on stock collateral at about 2 per cent. All customers having "long" stock carried for them were charged 6 per cent. legal interest. Some brokers obtained their loans on time at 3 to 4 per cent. per annum for six months.

It is immaterial whether a customer buys 100 shares of stock at 20, costing $2,000, or 100 shares at 150, costing $15,000. For $1,000 margin the banker-broker will buy 100 shares of either of them. A decline in price is likely to be as great in one as in the other.

If a man puts up $1,000 margin and buys 100 shares costing $15,000, he must pay interest on $14,000 as long as the stock is carried for him. Now, if the banker obtains money at 2 per cent. and charges 6 per cent., he makes an interest profit of 4 per cent. at the expense of his customer. This interest profit pays the banker-broker about $1.55 per day, $46.66 per month, $280 for six months and $560 for a year, if carried so long, which sometimes happens.

If a high priced stock is carried a long time the dividends the customer gets is an offset to the interest he has to pay. But this is neither here nor there between him and the banker, who gets money at one rate to carry the stock, and charges another rate for a big profit.

Suppose the banker-broker carries 100,000 shares for 30 days for customers on margins of $1,000 each, and the average cost of all this stock is $60 per share—100,000 shares at $60 is $6,000,-000. With interest at 2 per cent. the banker-broker gets the money for 30 days for $10,000; he charges the customers $30,000 and pockets $20,-000 for interest profits, besides $25,000 commission profits on the turn, buying and selling this 100,000 shares.

It is nothing unusual for the news tissues to report that one house "has just bought 30,000 of this," or that another house "has sold 30,000 shares of that within the past hour."

In times of activity the brokers make commission money rapidly and in large amounts. In times of dullness and stagnation many do not see a commission for days at a time.

A few houses combine stock brokerage with the purchase and sale of commercial paper. Their profits on discounts range from 4½ to 6½ per cent. on good prime notes, running from two to four months. Some houses do a business of from

$5,000,000 to $10,000,000 a year in this specialty alone, and their profits from it are very large.

STOCK HOUSE SOPHISTRY.

If the morality of stock speculation is called in question, the banker-broker will generally reply, "As we look at it, stocks are a commodity and to spread them among investors it is necessary to have dealings in them; otherwise no railroads could be built or improvements made." This is all well enough as applied to investors, but the fact is that often the entire capital stock of railroads are bought and sold over and over from week to week on margins for mere gambling profits, in which the stocks are not spread among actual investors at all.

Sometimes the banker is a convivial fellow and invites the boys out to take a nip, after business, then back to the office, with whiskey in his brain, the banker expounds how to do it. " Always buy when stocks are one or two points down and sell out and go short one or two points up, then cover your shorts and go long again one or two points down, that's the way to scoop the profits." All of which should be taken *cum grano salis.* The banker knows this system is a beautiful one to rope in frequent commissions, and that it is too often disastrous in scooping the whole margins of the other fellows.

WHO GETS THE MONEY?

The qustion is sometimes asked, who gets away with all the money that is fed into the Wall Street mill? Perhaps the following exhibit will show where many millions of it go :

Stock Exchange has Members.... ...	1,100
Produce " " "	2,500
Cotton " " "	500
Consolidated Stock, Oil and Mining Exchange	500
Bankers Associated with them, say....	1,000
Total	5,600

If we put the annual private and family expenses of these 5,600 brokers and their associates at $2,500 (a low estimate) each, it would make a total of $14,000,000.

Then there are the rents of the banker-broker offices, the clerk hire and all the other expenses to be paid before there is anything left to live on and to accumulate a fortune from. The number of offices and average expense each might be classified as follows :

		Average Expense.	Total.
Stock Offices, say..	300...	$10,000....	$3,000,000
Produce Offices, say...........	300...	2,500....	750,000
Stocks and Oil ...	200...	2,000....	400,000

Cotton Offices. ... 100... $2,500 .... $250,000

Total private living expenses brought
    down 14,000,000

Grand total................$18,400,000

This $18,400,000 represents annual expenses, and is, of course, only a small part of the big sums the bankers and brokers get to add to their wealth of hundreds of thousands and millions of dollars, leaving the money taken out of speculation by interested capitalists who are not bankers and brokers and the money fed into the bucket shops out of the case altogether.

There are probably not less than 15,000 persons —bankers, brokers, clerks, messengers, etc.—who get their living in one way or another out of the transactions at all these Exchanges. Where, oh! where does all the money come from? Does it not come from the speculators who feed their money into the hopper of the Wall Street mill?

CHAPTER XXV.

THE MARKET.

IN the Spring of 1886 the outbreak of the trans-
continental troubles and the great strikes on
the southwestern railroads caused a considerable·
decline in the market, which enabled capitalists to
pick up large lines of stocks at low figures to hold
for a large advance.

In the Summer and Fall the crops harvested
were generally good. The railway earnings were
large and increasing. General prospects of all kinds
of business and trade were favorable. The outlook was flattering for a prolonged bull market
which would put speculative values higher than
they have been for years.

The professional operators were all loaded up
for a long pull, and the speculative public were
coming in as buyers in large numbers. About the
middle of November the pork-packers' strike in
Chicago caused quite a slump in the prices of
Western stocks. The strike collapsed in a week
or ten days; then there was a recovery and a
strong market.

In November there was a wild speculation in
Consolidated California and Virginia mining stock,
which advanced from $2.50 to $50 a share.

During the Summer and early Fall the rates of foreign exchange favored an influx of gold from Europe. This helped speculation and made the market buoyant.

In the latter part of November the money market was working towards stringency. The surplus bank reserve, which a year before was about $65,000.000 above the legal limit, became reduced to less than $8,000,000 in December. Rates on call loans were advanced on some days to far above the legal interest. Gold ceased to flow this way, and the high rates on bills of exchange tended towards large exports of bullion back to Europe. These things operated to check speculation on the bull side.

With affairs in this shape, it is supposed that some of the largest operators sold out large amounts of stock to take profits, with a view of buying back their stocks at much lower prices. At all events, stocks became largely distributed in the hands of small holders. Big bears sold the market short, and for days previous to the middle of December prices were tending downward.

High interest rates for money is calculated to make margin speculators carry as few stocks as possible, except when there is a movement favorable to them. The banker-brokers charge legal interest, and in addition can charge their customers any higher rate they have to pay for money to carry stocks. Hence, with call loans ranging between 6 and 40 per cent., the bull customers having stocks carried for them on margins were on the anxious seat.

The climax was reached on the afternoon of December 14th, near the close of business, when the rate on call loans was manipulated up to one per cent. per day. What happened on the opening of business the next day is told by the *Morning Journal* of December 16th, thus:

THE RUSH TO SELL.

The wildest scenes in Wall Street since the terrible May panic of 1884, which carried down a dozen strong houses, were witnessed yesterday.

The greatest day's business in the history of the New York Stock Exchange was transacted. The sales of 1,096,509 shares of stock were reported by the ticker, but a fair share of the dealings were not recorded at all. It is estimated that the transactions foot up 1,600,000 shares.

The excitement was too mad for the trading to be kept track of. All the quotation reporters could do was to gather as many sales as they could and let the rest go entirely.

When the doors of the Stock Exchange were flung open in the morning and the gong was sounded to begin business, the tumble in prices began. The pressure to sell was tremendous. There was no buyers. Orders came in by telegraph from London, Chicago, St. Louis, Baltimore, Philadelphia, Washington, Boston and all throughout the country to sell.

A panic seemed to have seized upon speculators the whole length and breadth of the land. Pandemonium reigned on the floor of the Exchange. The great room was packed with brokers. Insanity in its most violent form seemed to have attacked the mass of men.

The brokers struggled and yelled and shook their order pads in making their bids and offers. The galleries were packed with spectators who came to see the wonderful sight. No one who viewed the frenzied crowd below could understand how any one made himself heard, much less understood.

Hats fell off the brokers' heads and were trampled under foot. There was no time to pick them up. Neckties came undone. The buttons were torn from cuffs. Button-holes in coats were ripped out. The brokers were pushed and crushed, but words could not be wasted in expostulation. Talk was too valuable for that. It was all needed to avert losses or secure profits.

One after another the prices dropped, and the lower they went the greater was the excitement. It looked as if the bottom could not be found for values. Wall Street seemed plunging into ruin. A day was feared worse than Black Friday of 1873, when men who came down town in the morning millionnaires went home at night paupers.

In the streets surrounding the Stock Exchange the same wildness reigned as on the floor. Men clad in the height of fashion and wearing the glossiest silk hats dashed back and forth in the pouring rain until they were as bedraggled as the sodden vagrants who are encountered at every turn in the financial mart begging for nickels and dimes to buy whisky. Their fortunes depended on their efforts. Money was wanted by hundreds of men to ward of disaster. They hurried from bank to bank and from money-lender to money-lender. They begged for it and offered the most extravagant prices for it. The lenders were filled with alarm and clutched their money-bags the tighter. They asked the most perfect security before they would make any loans.

On the floor the price for money was run up to 1 per cent. " over night," or for a single day. That was at the rate of 365 per cent. a year.

Baron L. Von Hoffman, the banker, sent into the Board the offer of half a million at the regular rate of 6 per cent. a year. The brokers grabbed for the money and thousands after thousands were taken. The action of Baron Von Hoffman ended the tremendous charges of the greedy money-lenders and marked a turn in the tide.

It allayed fear and the excitement subsided. With the departure of the wildness prices began to improve. The day of terror went out with prices ascending. A great deal of apprehension remain-

ed, and many a man who was rich the day before was left to the reflection that another day of
descending values would make him penniless.
Lights were burning brightly in hundreds of offices
in Wall Street, and clerks were struggling with
great masses of figures when the *Journal* went to
press this morning.

The Windsor Hotel was packed with brokers
and operators and people who came out of curios-
ity last night. It is the financial rendezvous in
the evening, and the talk was of nothing but the
events of yesterday and the probabilities for to-
day.

The decline on this day was from $\frac{1}{2}$ to $9\frac{1}{2}$ per
cent. right through the list, and the total decline
on this and previous days was from 10 to 15 per
cent.

One of the truly good and pious men of the
market, after it was over, said :

" The situation is cleared up by the break. It
was expected, and the principal operators sold out
their stocks several days ago."

A prominent room-trader said :

"I am a bull now. The break was what the
market needed and did it a heap of good. You
can tell your friends they can buy almost anything and make money. Wall Street can be banked in when it will go through an experience like
to-day's in the shape it did."

The " principal operators " took their profits and

stood out from under in time, of course. They always do. But what "a heap of good" the break did the thousands of lambs who were wiped out, it would be hard to tell.

THE AFTER GOSSIP.

One prominent bear was said to have cleared $350,000 out of the break.

A lady who risked her principal in a certain stock had $48,000 profits in sight a few days before. The panic wiped her out clean, principal and profits.

A gentleman had $18,000 in sight on $3,000 of margin. He waited too long and his profits and margin disappeared in the whirlpool.

The club men suffered severely. A gentleman stated that of over 100 men he knew personally, to meet at Delmonico's or on Wall Street in the day time, not one of them knew where they were going to get a hundred dollars for the holidays.

One Club, whose members were connossieurs in rare wines and liquors, were compelled to resort to cheaper wines or do without. A story was told of a row between a member and the steward of the Club. It seems that the steward, at the suggestion of the member, entrusted him some time before with the savings of a lifetime for an investment that was to bring in a fortune. Result, the money vanished in the vortex of the maelstrom, leaving the steward stranded.

The panic caught up about all the small speculators, men who margined up on from 100 to 2,500
shares. It gobbled them up bodily without leaving
them enough to buy a midday lunch.

One old Wall Street *habitue*, who had seen all
the panics since 1873, said: " This one did more
harm than any of the others. Its victims may be
counted by the thousand, as in the whole list of
his speculative acquaintances, he had only met
one man that was not wiped out, and lost all the
profits and capital he had been nursing for months.
The one lucky man had closed out his accounts
the week before to go abroad."

THE AFTER MARKET.

The large inside operators improved their opportunity to pick up and recover another large line
of stocks around the bottom prices of the panic.
Values improved again and the talk and rumors
were all in favor of a big bull market to come.

Then the Inter-State Commerce bill in Congress;
the Pacific Railroad Seventy Year Extension Fund-
ing bill, and the Russian, Turkey-Franco-German
war cloud, with the subsequent great labor strikes
among the coal-handlers and 'longshoremen came'
up as disturbing elements, causing a halting and
irregular market.

At every session of Congress, expected action,
affecting railroads, land grants and United States
mail subsidies, is brought in as a bug-a-boo

to affect the stock market favorable to the de-
sires of the men who run it. Every little thing
occurring on the financial-political horizon is taken
advantage of to hoodwink outside speculators.
If the sources of the trickery and rumors originated, to lead and mislead the public, were traced
to the fountain head and exposed, the result
would be astounding, that such men could occupy
the social positions they do. It would make even
a horse laugh.

The sympathy which exists between the speculative markets of America and Europe is easily
explained. The English, the French, the Dutch
and the Germans are great speculative commercial gamblers. They deal enormously in American securities, because the interest and dividends
on good bonds and stocks are larger, and the market fluctuations wider than on their securities at
home. Hence, any political or warlike complica-
tion which causes them to throw over their own
and American stocks reacts on our own Exchanges,
as well as on the Bourses of London, Paris, Frankfort, Vienna and Berlin.

It is well known to political observers that
France is biding her time, and itching, to wipe
out the disaster of Sedan, by the recovery of the
Provinces of Alsace–Lorraine. The first effect of
a European war scare is to cause holders to turn
their foreign securities into money and await
events.

With things in this shape, our market in January, 1887, was adversely affected by the large sales of American stocks in London for English and Continental account. This, with the alternate war and peace rumors, made the market very irregular in New York.   •

A large amount of American stocks are listed at the London Exchange, and that is the European market for our securities. It should also be borne in mind that the difference between New York and London time is five hours. With business hours the same, from 10 A. M. to 3 P. M., the latter Exchange is just closing as the former is opening.

On January 24th there was a war panic in London, caused by alleged advices and selling orders from Paris and Berlin. This made the former place the financial centre of the war fever. The heavy selling of Americans there brought a serious decline in prices, and so intimidated London holders of our securities that they in turn sold heavily in New York on the same day.

Private cable advices had been received in New York, and at the commencement of business the first quotations opened off from $1\frac{1}{2}$ to 2 per cent. below the previous day's closing, right through the list, and a further decline in some instances of 1 per cent. followed.

The panic arose from rumors that France was moving troops towards the frontier, and was buying horses abroad for the use of the army. A denial of these rumors by Gen. Boulanger, the French Minister of War, caused a sudden revulsion from selling to buying stocks back again.

At the opening of business the next day, at both London and New York, prices were jumped up 2 per cent. at first quotations. The decline of the previous day was recovered almost at a bound. The panic was nothing but a financial somersault for stock-jobbing purposes. And as the unexpected always happens to those who least expect it, the bears on both sides of the big pond had a lively time climbing to cover their shorts put out on the strength of the war rumors.

The passage of the Inter-State Commerce bill had been discounted. The subsidence of the war scare sent stocks booming upward again. The fizzling out of the labor strikes also helped for a time to make the market strong and buoyant. But there soon came another halt.

By reason of adverse legislative action, inimical to the wishes of the Chancellor, Prince Bismarck had previously dissolved the German Parliament. The German elections for new members was made a factor in speculation, both here and in Europe, as having a bearing on the question of peace or war.

Something always comes up that enables the leaders of the market in New York, and their allies in Europe to act on advance information, and to trade in their stocks for profitable turns. The profits, of course, have to come out of the pockets of the crowd, whose only recourse is to " wait till the clouds roll by."

The elections resulted in a victory and vindication for the master mind of Europe, probably assuring peace for awhile at least, and was construed as favorable to the interests of speculative finance. Stocks were boomed up 2 or 3 per cent. on the strength of it, giving the knowing ones another opportunity for profitable trading. Then the market was made to slump down again to enable them to get back their stock.

Now; March 1st, '87, all hands are waiting for the expiration of the 49th Congress. Then all fears of legislation unfavorably affecting railways and stock speculation will be at an end for a long time to come. And then, too, if the wise men of Wall Street are to be believed, the biggest bull market ever seen is to be gradually worked up.

The rapid recovery of the country from its long period of depression has naturally led to the conclusion that a long season of inflation must follow. If the financial doctors are right, and a big boom does come, it will be interrupted by many a slump, engineered by the " big men " to realize profits and recover their stocks for succeeding bulges and reactions.

The average speculator will do well to let the

bear side alone. He will do still better to make his margins 30 per cent. strong. And he will do superlatively better still to run at the least sign of danger when he has a profit in sight.

As it was in the time preceding the big bull market of 1881–2, when reams upon reams of stock, much of it not worth the paper it was written on, was floated and eagerly grabbed up, just so it is now. A vast amount of worthless stock is being put out in Wall Street. In a boom almost anything, having an appearance of value, will sell. Good stocks on the advance will drag poor stocks up with them, and *vice versa* in a declining movement the worthless stuff helps to drag good stocks, having real merit, down in value.

It is to the interest of the insiders to boom up everything, good, doubtful, and worthless. When the bubble can be inflated no farther, they are cunning enough to slowly feed out all they have to sell and to pocket their money. Then the final culmination of the great bull market will be the old, old story of 1883 and 1884, when tens of thousands of the outside public, who had been enticed in by illusions, were left stranded. Then, too, all those who rely on the superior wisdom of their whilom banker and broker friends, to " hold on, the market will turn up again and you will come out all right," will be all the worse roasted the longer they " hold on," by the ruthless raids of the bears to destroy the value of their property.   And some of these bears may be the very same fellows who enticed in and pocketed bull profits out of these very innocents.

CHAPTER XXVI.

THE ROAD TO SUCCESS.

THE ability to command unlimited money and to form pools and combinations of hundreds of millions of dollars is what makes the Wall Street kings so irresistible. They can make the market what they will. Against them the general public, as speculators, have not the ghost of a chance. Here and there a few friends of this or that manipulator of stocks may be let into the confidence of the inner circle and be allowed to operate with more or less sure results.

The public in general are the victims, the prey and the meat, so to speak, of the money farmers of Wall Street. To get the public to come in as buyers is necessary to the successful ending of their schemes. These schemes always culminate in the victims being left in a fix from which there is no escape without more or less serious losses, if not absolute ruin.

Hence those who have only enough of this world's goods to support themselves and families in comfort, with no surplus to risk in a game of chance, have no business in Wall Street. Their only safe road to wealth is to scratch from morning to night at some honest employment and save every penny.

To the person who wishes to invest for income only there are certain classes of stocks which are almost as safe as a mortgage. These are the stocks of roads leased to other prosperous corporations, which guarantee interest on their bonds and dividends on their stocks.

The Rensselaer and Saratoga Railroad, for instance, is leased to the Delaware and Hudson Canal Company, which guarantees interest on bonds, and 8 per cent. dividends on the stock. The Delaware and Hudson Canal Company must pay these charges before it can pay anything on its own bonds and stocks. Good stocks like this, which are guaranteed, are seldom in the market for sale; their quotations are very high and they are not subject to speculative fluctuations like other stocks, because they are so closely held by investors, for the income they bring. Some of the strongest railway corporations have leased lines on which interest and dividends are guaranteed, but their price is so high it brings the income on their cost down to 4 or 5 per cent. on those paying 8 or 9 per cent. dividends. This, however, is offset by the stock being exempt from taxes. They are seldom reported in the market except on a "wash" to get a price quoted.

The outsider should never sell stocks short. Only professional operators, who thoroughly understand all the tricks of stock dealings, can hope to succeed on the short side. Professional bears are themselves often caught in corners and lose more ammunition than they could have hoped to make.

To be safe a man should never speculate on a margin. Fifty per cent. is called a strong margin, but even that is frequently wiped out if the stock has been bought high up and is held too long in a falling market. On a weak margin a man may lose it at the first venture. Or he may take minimum profits and losses for a long time, but sooner or later he will get caught by the unexpected that will swallow all he has, if it does not leave him in debt to his brokers.

No prudent man or woman should speculate for catchpenny profits of one, two or three hundred dollars on each 100 shares. Small successes only lead on to heavy set-backs that eat up all profits and often a big hole in the margin.

The worst thing prudent or imprudent people can do is to hang around the banker-broker offices. They are subject to the manifold influences which there prevail to warp and pervert common-sense, discretion and good judgment, and which too often lead them into traps and pitfalls.

The banker-brokers are there to make money. No one should be deceived by their oily gammon, for under it all they are ravenous for commissions. Of course they would be only too glad to have their customers make money every time. But they know things don't work that way, and so, if they can make money for themselves, it is all one to them whether their clients can or not. The tape speculator soon becomes a confirmed gambler, and as hardened and heartless as the blood-suckers who feed upon him.

People should never buy stocks, either for speculation or investment, after the price has been boomed up 20, 30, or 40 per cent. above the bottom of a previous decline. That is the very time when those who have inflated prices are singing their sweetest and most alluring notes to induce people to come as buyers. They are ready to sell out through various brokers so that their operations cannot be traced.

The good years and the bad years follow periodically in the stock market like the seven years of plenty and the seven years of famine in Egypt. Usually there are two, three or four prosperous years with crops and business all good, then there comes bad years of poor crops, poor business and depression. All these things should be remembered and calculated on by those who meddle with the stock market.

To sum up, the outsider should
1. Never short the market.
2. Never buy on top of the booms.
3. Never buy on a margin.
4. Keep away from stock office influences and street gossip.

5. Operate only as an investor for dividend income.

6. Only buy low after severe declines.

By following these rules and buying good stocks, any man who has surplus money and has patience to wait months or a year or two for results can make an enormous interest on his investment over and above the dividend income he will receive quarterly or semi-annually.

The family man should invest his money to secure a sure and certain support for his family. He should use only surplus money he can spare in stock operations. Stocks which are considered good sound income payers one year, may the next year pass their dividends, and suffer a heavy decline in price through deceptive book-keeping or by being too closely paralleled by a new road fighting for business. In such a contingency a man should be prepared to wait years for the payment of dividends to be resumed, and for the price of the stock to advance to at least the price it cost him. Everything comes to him who waits, in the stock market, unless—unless it is worthless past redemption.

People should keep away from Wall Street and watch the market from a distance, through the newspaper reports, for great depressions and declines in prices. Then, with values from 30 to 50 per cent. off from the top of a previous boom, will be the time to look all around the business horizon. If crops are growing, are they likely to be good? If crops have been harvested, have we a large surplus for export? Is there a large shortage of European crops of which we have a surplus? Are we exporting or importing gold? Are the railway earnings large and increasing, and are the roads at peace or at war?

Having cast a mental horoscope of the near future, and if satisfied that the most of these things are favorable to an improvement in business interests, a man can come in and buy good stocks with confidence.

He should buy dividend payers. If he buys several hundred or thousand shares, he should make good selections of stocks of several different Companies. Then he will not have all his eggs in one basket. If one stock does not do well, he may achieve good results on the others. He should buy only what he can pay for. Then he should take his stocks away, and have them recorded in his name in the offices of the different Railway Companies. Having done this, he should lock them up in his strong box, or place them in the vaults of a Safe Deposit Company. Then he should go away and keep away from Wall Street, and watch and wait patiently for months or a year or more for the good time coming. It will come sooner or later.

The man who has bought his stocks comparatively low, and has paid for them, can afford to

see the price go, temporarily, 10 or 20 per cent.
under the price he paid. He should never be
frightened into throwing over his stocks. It is a
common trick to work on people's fears, and
freeze them out, so that other men can get the
stocks at a low price to hold for a big advance.

The position of a man who has paid for what he
holds is impregnable. The bears may do their
worst ; but they cannot hurt him, if he will only
keep cool, and laugh at their fictions.

The good time coming will come at last. It
may be within three months or it may take one or
two years. Aided by natural causes, stocks will
go booming or will be put up by main force by
artificial manipulation 20, 30 or 40 per cent.
Then is the time for the holder of stocks to come
down into Wall Street and dump them on the
market. The outsider should be sure to sell out
and take his profits before the big insiders can sell
out theirs and go short for a decline.

Having sold out, a man should gather up his
principal and profits and run away. He should
not wait a minute for his banker to talk him into
another venture. Get away from Wall Street and
keep away from its influences until another great
periodical decline comes around. Then go into
the market and invest again as near bottom prices
as can be guessed at, and record and put away the
stocks and leave the Street until another big bull
market sends prices kiting again.

This process, if repeated in all the big declines and advances, will, in the course of ten or twenty years, result in a big fortune from small beginnings.

A man can always prophesy after an event. Here was what could have been done. In January, 1885, Delaware, Lackawanna and Western could have been bought around 83. The equivalent of 100 shares at 83 is $8,300. In December following the price was $135 a full share. 100 shares at 135 is $13,500. This, if bought and sold at the right times, would have yielded a profit of about $5,200. In addition, during that time three dividends were paid on it, two of 2 per cent. and one of 1¼ per cent., making $575 in dividends, which, added to the profit, made a total net gain of $5,750 after paying commissions, all made within one year.

In the same year Lake Shore was below 51 in the Spring or Summer. The next fall it was in the nineties, and once crossed par in 1886, a gain of over $4,000 on 100 shares. Union Pacific in 1884 advanced from 28 to 58 in three months, a gain of $3,000 in the value of 100 shares.

It is always more safe to buy the dividend payers. But sometimes a judicious selection from among the Fancies will pay a tremendous profit. O. T. in 1884 was down to $625 for 100 shares. In less than two years it was, at one time, worth $3,800, a difference of $3,175.

Then there was Ohio Central, the poorest stuff

on the whole list, down to 12½ cents a share in 1885, 100 shares for $12.50. It boomed in less than a year to $200 for 100 shares, a gain of 1,500 per cent.

The cheap stocks are very risky to meddle with for investment. By bad management and inherent rottenness, they may be forced into the hands of receivers, or sold under foreclosure for defaults of interest or principal on bonds. If the sale does not cover the bonded indebtedness, the stock is wiped out and annihilated.

Great discretion must be exercised in the selection of investment stocks. A few years ago the Louisville and Nashville, the Central Pacific and the Union Pacific were all 6 and 7 per cent. dividend payers, and sought after for the income. But one after the other their dividends were passed, and they dropped down among the " Fancies " to be kicked around by both bull and bear.

At one time the Vanderbilt stocks were considered the safest investments on the lists. But times changed and dividends were passed on Michigan Central and Canada Southern temporarily. The Lake Shore and N. Y. Central had their business cut into by parallel lines, causing the former to suspend dividends for a time, while that of the latter was reduced one-half.

The following list of stocks with the dividends they pay per annum, are, in the order named, about the most reliable, so far as things can be seen on the surface.

Dividend rate, per cent.

Chicago and Northwestern, pref....	7
Illinois Central	8
Chicago and Alton, pref................	8
Chicago, Burlington and Quincy.........	8
Chicago, Rock Island and Pacific.........	7
Pullman Palace Car.....................	8
Delaware, Lackawanna and Western.......	7
Chicago and Alton, common.....	7
Chicago, Milwaukee and St. Paul, pref.....	7
Chicago and Northwestern, common......	6
St. Paul Omaha, pref...................	6
St. Paul, Minneapolis and Manitoba......	7
St. Paul and Duluth, pref..............	7 .
Delaware and Hudson Canal Co........ .	5
Oregon Railway and Navigation.........	6
Lake Shore and Mich. Southern, last div..	2
N. Y. Central Hudson River...........	4
Long Island	4
Chicago, Milwaukee & St. Paul, common..	5

The above list are mostly active stocks which fluctuate more or less widely. Leased roads on whose stocks dividends are guaranteed are not quoted, because such are too closely held for incomes to be active in the market. The New York Central Hudson is intrinsically a very valuable property, but is crippled as a big dividend payer by the incubus of the West Shore. The real estate of the Central Hudson in New York and other cities and towns along its line is estimated as worth at least $100,000,000, besides rolling stock and equipments.

It is the investor who buys good stocks when the price is low, pays for them in full, and keeps away from the market, who makes money and grows rich.

It is the tape speculator and hanger-on around the brokers' offices, who is manipulated in and out of the market, both on the long and short sides, and milked by his banker for frequent commissions, and interest on carrying stocks when money is cheap, who nine times out of ten eventually loses all the property he has in the world. The infatuation of gambling is on him. He is imbued with the hallucination that he can recover all his losses by a few lucky strokes. And if his or her friends do not step in and institute proceedings in lunacy, to have the money remaining placed in trust, he or she will keep on until they go clean dead broke.

In the Fall of 1886 it was stated by one of the Wall Street organs, that out of a given number of houses on "the Street," not one of their customers had closed out their accounts, during the past sixteen years, with a profit in the end.

One customer was reported who had paid his brokers over $10,000 in commissions, and who closed out his accounts with a balance of only $350 left to his name.

The following list shows the highest, lowest and closing prices for the year 1886, and the closing price on March 1, 1887.

	1886. Highest.	1886. Lowest.	1886. Closing.	1887. Closing Bid. March 1st.
Atlantic and Pacific	13⅝	7	11⅞	11⅝
Canadian Pacific	73	62¾	67⅜	60
Central Pacific	51¾	38	43¼	35¾
Cameron Coal	44	9	43¾	44½
Canada Southern	71½	34¾	63¾	58¾
Chicago and Northwest	120⅝	104¼	115⅛	114⅝
" " " pref	144	135	140	141
Chicago, Rock Island and Pacific	131	120⅛	126⅛	126
Chicago, Burlington and Quincy	141¾	128¾	136	137½
St. Paul	99	82⅝	90¾	90⅞
" pref	125¾	116	118¼	120
Cincinnati, Washington and Baltimore	6¾	2½	6	5
" " " " pref	12	5	10	8¾
Colorado Coal	41¼	21	40	37¼
Consolidated Gas	111	74⅞	80½	83⅛
Hocking Valley	45	26⅞	37¾	35
Cleveland, Columbus, Cincinnati and Ind.	75½	43½	64½	......
Delaware, Lackawanna and Western	143¾	115	136⅞	134¼
Delaware and Hudson Canal Co.	108½	87¼	103⅝	101⅝
Denver and Rio Grande	35¾	21¼	32¼	24¾
East Tennessee, Virginia and Georgia	6½	½		......
" " " " " new	18⅞	11	16⅝	13¼
" " " " " 1st pref	83½	67¾	79¼	75
" " " " " 2d pref	35¾	28	31¾	25
Fort Worth and Denver City	25½	15	25	25
Green Bay and Winona	14⅜	8	13½	12½
Indiana, Bloomington and Western	28⅞	12	17	......
Lake Shore	100⅝	76⅛	96⅛	94¼
Lake Erie and Western	18¾	7¼	13	......
" " " assessment paid	22¼	14¾	19½	......
Long Island	100	80⅞	94	......
Louisville and Nashville	69	33⅛	66⅜	60¾
Michigan Central	98¾	61½	93⅞	87½
Manhattan Consolidated	175	120	158¼	......
Memphis and Charleston	69⅛	29	59	55½
Milwaukee, Lake Shore and Western, pref	103	50¼	92⅞	102
Minneapolis and St. Louis	23⅞	16¼	19¾	.. ...
" " " pref	52⅛	40½	44	42

	1886.			1887.
	Highest.	Lowest.	Closing.	Closing Bid. March 1st.
Missouri, Kansas and Texas............	37⅞	21	33¼	30⅞
Missouri Pacific....................................	119	100¾	108⅜	108
New Jersey Central.......	64	42¼	55⅝	67
New York Central......	117⅜	98¼	113¼	112¼
New York, Chicago and St. Louis..............	17¼	4½	14⅞	6¼
" " " " pref...... ..	31	11	28	18⅞
New York and New England..................	68⅝	30⅞	55	60⅛
Nashville, Chattanooga and St. Louis..........	105⅜	43¼	88	83
New York, Lake Erie and Western.............	38⅜	22⅞	34¼	33½
" " " " pref......	81⅜	50½	73	71½
New York, Susquehanna and Western.........	12⅜	6	12	12⅝
" " " " pref...	33⅞	17⅞	33	35
Northern Pacific...........	31⅛	22	27¾	27¾
" " pref..	66½	53¼	61⅝	58¼
Norfolk and Western......	27¼	8½	22¾	20¼
" " " pref....................	59⅝	25	52⅝	47¼
Ontario and Western...............	22⅞	15	20	17¼
Oregon and Trans................................	38	25	33¾	31⅞
Oregon Railway and Navigation..................	109⅞	93	104	101¼
Ohio and Mississippi............	35⅜	19⅞	29¼	27
Pacific Mail..............	67	45¾	51	54⅝
Peoria, Decatur and Evansville..................	34⅝	16½	31½	35
Richmond and West Point......................	77⅝	27½	71	74
Reading.....................................	59	18⅞	36½	36
St. Paul and Omaha	55	35¾	48⅞	48
St. Paul and Omaha, pref.	116⅝	97	109	108½
St. Paul, Minneapolis and Manitoba..	124⅞	106¾	115	115
St. Paul and Duluth.......	67	37	58	60½
" " " pref.....................	115	99¾	106½	......
St. Louis and San Francisco.	37⅞	17	31⅞	32¼
" " " pref...............	77¼	37½	65	65½
Southern Pacific.............	41½	30½	36⅝	......
Texas Pacific...........	25	7½	24½	......
" " assessments paid........	28⅜	17½	24⅝	27½
Union Pacific...........	68¼	44¼	61⅜	57
Western Union...	80⅛	60⅞	75¼	73⅞
Wabash, St. Louis and Pacific, pref......	22⅞	14	14	17⅞
" " " " " receipts	41⅛	23⅞	35½	30

CHAPTER XXVII.

POSSIBILITIES OF RAILWAY FINANCE.

TO the right sort of man who has millions of money as a basis; one whose head is cool and level at all times; one who has great subtlety in manipulation; who is thoroughly heartless and unscrupulous in the means to attain an end; who upon occasion can buy up political and judicial favors; one who can buy controlling interests in great railway lines and has the directory in the hands of his own creatures; who can have the railway reports of his companies cooked to order for speculative effect; one who is cunning in invention of plausible rumors; who can water his stocks and conceal his hand; one who is as crafty and ruthless as a pirate in the inception and final culmination of his schemes: to such a man, with a long career before him, unchecked by legal interference and left to work out his designs undisturbed by socialists, communists and anarchists, the possibilities of speculative railway finance are gigantic and unlimited.

Given, then, that such a man could have one hundred million of dollars for a beginning, and could have one hundred years of active life to manipulate the stock market—what then?

Why, profiting by the experience of the most successful Wall Street kings, who had made great fortunes and left vast estates, he would adopt their methods and improvise new ones of his own. He would avoid the practices which so often engulfed the great bears in irretrievable disaster.

He could employ brokers by the scores and hundred to execute his orders with entire secrecy. He could have a news and rumor-mill of his own, to allure the public into the market, or to freeze them out as suited his purpose.

By buying 51 shares out of every 100 he could get control of railway corporation after corporation, and elect himself and his own creatures to the directory. He could manipulate the stock of his companies for stock-jobbing profits without the least regard to the interests of the other stockholders.

If he wished to depress prices of good stock to buy them in low, he could pass the dividends and institute cut-rate wars. If it were non-dividend stocks he wished to buy cheap he could accomplish the same object by causing a default in the payment of interest on their bonds. When he had bought all the stock he wanted, he could send prices booming upward by resuming the payment of dividends and interest on stocks and defaulted bonds.

If he wished to buy up a railroad cheap which was in default in the payments on its bonded debt, he could purchase a majority of the indebtedness, and by proceedings in foreclosure and sale could buy in the road for perhaps less than the incumbrances on it, thereby wiping out all its stock capital. Then by reorganizing a new Company and circulating news of great improvements to be made to rehabilitate the road, he could float an immense amount of new bonds and stock, and inflate their prices as high as a kite to sell them out to the lambs of Wall Street.

The disastrous experience of such bears as Daniel Drew, Jacob Little and others would admonish him never to short the market to be cornered by opposition combinations. He would allow bears the utmost latitude in destroying values when he wished to buy low. When booming the market he would encourage the bears to sell stocks short by loaning them, through his brokers, all the stock they wanted to make their deliveries. When a large short interest had accumulated he would call in all his loaned stock, corner the bears, exact high loaning rates and make them bid prices away up against themselves, while he was using them as catspaws to rake his own chestnuts (profits) out of the fire.

With his hundred million of dollars as a beginning he could buy and pay for a million or a million and a half shares of stocks, at the bottom of the big declines, and slowly sell them out on the top of the booms at profits of from 20 to 50 per cent. Some years he could repeat the process two or three times a year.

If he followed up all his opportunities to trade in his stocks, and to buy and sell on all the big declines and advances, he would, with the profits of all his periodical sheep shearings : the dividends on his stocks, the interest on the bonds he would accumulate and on the money he would save by tax evasions, be worth at the end of 100 years a fortune more colossal than the present combined wealth of all the money kings of Europe.

He might acquire the control of all the railroads in the country, with surplus wealth enough to compass the ownership of the whole city of New York and entire towns and villages besides. But what of the vast multitudes who, all this time, had been bringing grist to his mill? Why! "The public be d—d!"

CHAPTER XXVIII.

EXEGESIS.

IN the history of antiquity we may read of the riches and glory of Solomon and of the mag· nificent wealth of gold and jewels with which he adorned the sanctuary. We may have a glimpse of the opulence and luxury of the ancient Romans.

But we need not go back beyond Anno Domini for faint glimmers of the game of finance—if game there was.

We have the evidence of Holy Writ that "the Son of Man drove the money changers out of the Temple."

We have the inspiration of the Almighty that " he who hasteth to be rich shall not be inno-cent."

That "it shall be easier for a camel to go through the eye of a needle than for a rich man " (rich men like these) " to enter into the kingdom of Heaven."

And, " What shall it profit a man if he gain the whole world and lose his own soul ?"

If the usual closing exercises were to follow in such a connection as that in the general scope of this work, it ought to be that all right-minded people should pray that from the wiles of man

and the devil, from ruined homes, from demoralization and other widespread evils of margin gambling " may the good Lord deliver us."

But what is to become of those fellows who have
fattened, and accumulated enormous fortunes by
delusion and artifice, out of the very life-blood,
so to speak, of tens and hundreds of thousands of
their fellow creatures? They want to gain the
whole earth, but they don't want to go to the
infernal regions.

In this dilemma a mighty expounder of the
theory of evolution steps in with an entire dis-
belief in the doctrine of eternal punishment.
Hence, with no hell, no fire, no brimstone in prospect, these lords and mighty men of Wall Street,
relieved of future terrors, will go on erecting
palaces cemented by the misery of their victims,
and living in a style of regal or semi-regal splen-
dor, with retinues of servants and an entourage
paid for by profits wrung from their dupes by artifice and cunning.

They will cling to the image of gold until the
last. But how will it be when the Angel Gabriel
shall sound his last trump? Can they elude the
vigilance of St. Peter? Will they be turned
away from the portals of Paradise with the order,
" Procul, O procul este, profani!" only to meet
the agent of his Satanic majesty to be conducted
to the other place? Who knows? They don't;
but they risk it for the shimmer of gold.

CHAPTER XXIX.

RICH MEN OF EUROPE.

THE ENORMOUS WEALTH OF THE ROTHSCHILDS AND THE NOBLES.—WEALTHY DUKES.

FOR many years the richest individual in all Russia was Herr Steiglitz. When he retired from affairs in 1860 he held property to the value of nearly £2,000,000. But the richest men in the land of the Czars at the present time are the two Nobel brothers. They are of Swiss origin. While traveling through interior Russia they saw thousands of acres of land aglow with the light of oil gas. They at once purchased entire districts of the apparently worthless fields, sunk oil wells, and now control more petroleum than any other concern in the world. Their wealth is really beyond calculation, though a correspondent thinks that £80,000,000 is not an extravagant estimate.

It is to the Rothschilds, however, that belongs the honor of being richest among men. Their united properties—and their properties must be considered as united from their peculiar family and business relations—pass even beyond the mil-

lions. In the last twelve years they have loaned
to certain European governments nearly £90,000,-
000. Their lordly power is shown in a modern
instance. In 1866 the Prussian government demanded an indemnity of £5,000,000 from the city
of Frankfort. The head of the Rothschild house
in that city sent word to Count Bismarck that if
an attempt was made to force the levy he would
break every. bank in Berlin, and Bismarck was
compelled to give way. The enormous wealth of
the Rothschilds is doubly remarkable from the
fact that the family was totally unknown a century ago. Inferior only to the Rothschilds are
the Baring brothers, who have " at instantaneous
command " £60,000,000. It is noteworthy that
the Barings owe their commercial rise to an
American, Mr. William Bigelow, of Philadelphia,
who, many years ago, had the house appointed
the American Agency in London.

Among the richest of moderns is the Czar of
Russia, who enjoys from his personal estate an
income of £2,000,000. The Sultan of Turkey is
allowed for the support of his court over £1,200,-
000 ; in addition to this he has a private income
of £1,000,000. The Emperor of Austria is granted
a yearly allowance of £2,500,000.

There are several noblemen in England who
have immense wealth at their command. The
Dukes of Buccleuch, Devonshire and Norfolk, and
the Marquis of Bute have each of them rent rolls

of £400,000 per annum. The Duke of Portland, who died recently, left unentailed property of over £2,000,000. The greater part of his palace was constructed underground. His banquet-hall, ball-room, riding-school, and a number of superb guest rooms are veritable tunnels, decorated in a fashion so splendid as to seem, when described, like a story of the Magi.

Richer even than any of these millionaires is the Duke of Westminster, who undoubtedly has the largest income of any individual in the world. His fortune lies largely in the diametrically opposite regions of London, known as the West End and Seven Dials. He owns acre upon acre of the most aristocratic domain in London, and his tenements cover miles in the worst slums in the world. His income passes the limit of the credible, and is said by some to amount to £10 a minute.—*London Times*.

RICH PEOPLE OF AMERICA.

Common report estimates the wealth of some of the richest people in this country at about the following figures :

	Estimated.
The combined wealth of the Astors.	$250,000 000
Cornelius Vanderbilt...............	115,000 000
W. K. Vanderbilt.......	100,000 000
Jay Gould..................	100,000 000
The four daughters of the late W. H. Vanderbilt combined......	42,000 000

Collis P. Huntington.............	$40,000 000
Charles Stanford.................	40,000 000
Mrs. Mark Hopkins........	30,000 000
Alexander Mitchell...............	30,000 000
Mrs. Hettie Greene..	30,000 000
Mrs. A. T. Stewart estate.........	25,000 000
E. D. Morgan estate.............	25,000 000
Moses Taylor estate.............	30,000 000
David Dows....................	15,000 000
Russell Sage...................	15,000 000
Robert Garrett.:...............	15,000 000
Fred Vanderbilt................	13,000 000
George Vanderbilt.............	12,000 000

Then there are the Mackays, the Fairs and
Sharons of California, the silver kings of Nevada,
the rich lumber men of the Northwest, the Pack-
ers and others of Pennsylvania, the millionaires
of New England, the Crockers and Standard Oil
people, with wealth ranging from ten to fifty millions each.

"Howard," in the *World*, says : " There are
hundreds of millionaires in New York of whom
the general public never heard. There are half a
hundred worth from two to five millions each,
and at least a score whose individual wealth may
be reasonably estimated anywhere from $25,-
000,000 to $50,000,000, concerning whom the
ordinary citizen is absolutely ignorant. Yet they
are men of affairs whose transactions affect commercial relations that belt the globe—whose busi-

ness conduct has something to do with every known industry in which mechanics, oil, light and fuel are factors."

"It used to be said throughout New England, 'The young men go to New York to seek a fortune.' Now, it is said, 'The men of the country, from the golden shores of California and the snow-clad hills of the Sierra Nevada range, from the cattle kings of the great middle lands to the coal barons and the petroleum princes of the Middle States, go to New York to spend their fortunes.'"

"Phenomenally rich and extraordinarily quiet about it, like all the others, like the oil men and the iron men, and the soap men and the stock speculators in California, they have come to this city as to a place of refuge, a place large enough to insure quiet, a place crowded enough to make desirable privacy certain."

Speaking of the opening night of the season at the Metropolitan Opera House, "Howard" further says: "It is a curious fact that the men who will to-morrow night occupy their boxes, are the actual possessors—not the representatives, mind you, but the actual possessors—of property; that is, real estate, bonds and stock of various names, estimated modestly in the stupendous sum of eight hundred millions of dollars, while millionaires and quintuple millionaires will be as plentiful in the opera house as pebbles in an aquarium."

The one million millionaires are so plenty that they do not count for as much now as a $5,000 man did a hundred years ago.

After W. H. Vanderbilt's death there was a rumor that a private inventory of his money and securities in the vaults of the Lincoln National Bank revealed a market value of $305,000,000 in personal property alone. But this was rumor only.

CHAPTER XXX.

THE INEQUALITIES OF TAXATION.

RAILWAY bonds are taxable as personal property, just as much as mortgages or money.
But of the thousands of millions of dollars in railway bonds, it is hardly probable that one-half in
amount of these bonds pays any tax whatever.
The desire to evade taxation and throw the public burdens on other people's shoulders is almost
universal. Men who will tell the truth in almost
everything else ; men whose word is said to be as
good as their bond, will fib and quibble to keep
down their taxes.

The richer a man is, particularly if he is a speculative gambler, the more prone he is to shirk his
just share, or evade taxes altogether.

Railway stocks are exempt in the hands of their
holders, for the reason that the roads pay local and
State taxes all along their lines. That is all right
and just enough. But stocks are too often made
a bulwark and shield behind which evasions are
made of taxable property to the amouut, in the
aggregate, of hundreds of millions of dollars,

sometimes even of millions and tens of millions in the hands of one man, or in an estate.

The consequence of this condition of affairs is, that every farmer, every owner of real property and every person who honestly gives a true account of his personal property for taxation, has to pay a largely increased tax-rate to make up the losses on the evasion of assessments. Many of these tax evaders are a thousand and ten thousand times more able to pay their equitable share out of their enormous surplus income, than are more honest people out of the proceeds of poorly requited toil and to the deprivation of personal comforts.

The New York *World* in its exposures of the tax evasions in 1886, says: " The poor who have a few hundreds laid by in savings banks for a rainy day, drawing 3 per cent. interest, must pay out of that meagre income $2\frac{29}{100}$ towards making up the deficiency caused by those who shirk their share of the city taxes. An instance of this injustice was demonstrated while the reporters were looking over the books. ———, a colored barber, who after many years had saved up and put in savings banks $3,000, on which he gets $90 a year interest, called, and, with tears in his eyes, paid $68.70 tax on his money, leaving him but $21.30. A widow having a few thousand dollars left her by her husband, was in a like position."

Poor people who have no real or personal property to be assessed, have to pay a grinding tax in

increased rents to landlords and in the enhanced
cost of provisions and clothing.

As a rule, especially in the country, every man's
word is taken as to the amount he is liable to be
taxed for. Occasionally a man who underrates
his property by a few hundreds or a few thousands
has his personal valuation put up to a high figure,
and is made to swear it down, if he can, or compelled to stand it. This is too often done to
gratify personal spite on the part of the assessor
or his friends, who put him up to it ; the assessor
always taking refuge under the plea that he is only
doing his duty ; and this too often when he knows
he is making mockery of his oath of office in knowingly allowing others to evade taxes to a far larger
amount.

This is all wrong. The law or the practice
should compel every one to verify his assessment
every time it is made ; then if he willfully per-
jures himself, let him take the consequences when
found out.

Ours is a free country. We want no harsh, ar-
bitrary, or despotic laws. Legislation should be
just, equitable and beneficent.

The huge speculative gamesters and their stool
pigeons in the New York markets should be
brought to book. They prey on the credulity
and grow enormously rich at the expense of
thousands of dupes. Many have overflowing coffers of money and taxable securities. Once a year

at the tax office it is nothing new to see millionaires shirk taxation under the plea that their personal property is all in stocks. Death, or some
other circumstance, reveals the fact that a deliber-
ate felony has been committed.

If these men will not bear their honest share of
the public burdens, then, in justice to the people
at large, let us have thumb-screw, star chamber
inquisition laws to take these high priests of the
great god Mammon by the throat and make them
disgorge without a chance of evasion.

There are scores on scores of bears in the stock
market. Small bears put up from $1,000 to
$10,000 as margin on short sales. Big bears put
up from $100,000 to $1,000,000 for the same
purpose. They are dealing in stocks to be sure,
but they don't own the stocks they sell. They
have none, and have no more claim to exemption
from assessment than if their money was in visible
real estate.

Their speculative interest is a mere gamble, a
bet that prices of that they sell, but did not have
to sell, will decline. Besides the margin put up,
prudent bears will have thousands or hundreds of
thousands of dollars in cash reserves for contin-
gencies. This money should be assessed, but
precious little of it ever pays any tax.

There are dealers in stocks and commercial
paper, which latter is taxable. They may be
carrying from $50,000 to $500,000 of these prom-

issory notes and bills of exchange. But the magic word stocks comes in, or " our liabilities exceed the value of our assets."

The tax dodger is indigenous to both city and country. They fall back on stocks, or unhesitatingly make affidavit that their debts exceed the value of their personal property, in whole or in part.

There are millions upon millions of dollars locked up in the safes of greedy Wall Street speculators that never pay one dollar of just taxation. These men are not ignorant. They are the sharpest and shrewdest men in the city. They study the law to evade it. They will pay thousands on thousands of dollars to unscrupulous lawyers to baffle justice. It is a luxury to rob the government and defraud the people.

A certain fixed sum is levied for State expenses, other fixed sums are wanted to sustain municipal governments in cities, and to pay expenses of towns and counties. It is evident that if the richer class shirk their due share, the greater part of the burden must fall on people who are least able to bear it.

Directly and indirectly this question affects everybody. An entire revision of the tax laws should not longer be delayed.

One instance revealed $30,000,000 of taxable railway bonds in the hands of one man, which was assessed for only a fraction of a million.

The king pin of all the capitalists for years paid no personal tax. The pressure of public opinion at last brought out an assessment of $1,000,000 which remained at that figure until after his death. Then his will revealed $33,000,-000 of clear palpable taxable personal property, which was bound up to be held as a trust fund. How much more was covered and concealed in a wonderful residuary estate, of which no public inventory was taken, is only known to those immediately interested.

According to the *World's* exposure, this great fund of $33,000,000 went on the assessment roll last year at only $8,000,000, an evasion of $25,-000,000. The failure to collect the tax on this sum in this one instance, in New York, increased the tax rate from $2.20 per $100 to $2.29 per $100, so that other taxpayers had to pay the taxes on this $25,000,000 that was dodged.

People estimated and known to be worth from five million to way up in the tens of millions, get off with a personal assessment of from $25,000 up to $500,000.

The banks assessed on their capital stock endeavor to shirk their share of the tax. They claim that under section 5,219 of the Banking Act, passed in the sixties, a bank's stock should not be assessed against the bank as a corporation, but against the shareholders individually. A majority of the banks brought suit against the city to restrain it from collecting the tax.

Seventy-five banks were assessed on an aggregate capital of $60,746,294, representing 882,000 shares, which were held by 21,946 shareholders.

If bank shares were to be assessed against the individual holders of such shares, then the city, it is alleged, would lose almost the entire tax available therefrom, because holders would then claim, as it is done in thousands of cases, that their debts exceed their assessable personal property.

There are scores of men within the arena of speculation who have grown wealthy, if not enormously rich, some out of commissions, others by profits filched from the pockets of deluded fools. Many of these fellows who have grown rich by immunity do not contribute a dollar of personal tax, or pay anything for the privileges and protection they enjoy under our National, State and municipal government.

In New York city, during the Fall and Winter of 1886-7, the *World* brought to light and exposed about $100,000,000 of personal property in the hands of private individuals, in estates, city railroad and gas light companies, which was taxable, but evaded taxation.

This sum if assessed would have brought in a tax of about $2,000,000. The *World's* facts and figures lead to the irresistible conclusion that there are hundreds of millions of dollars of personal property which escapes assessment.

Of all great American fortunes, that of the Astors was undoubtedly one of the most honorably acquired, and bears the most honest share of the burdens of taxation. This is so because the great bulk of the Astor property is in real estate. A large tax is also paid on personal property.

The Astor fortune originated in honorable trade. Then it increased rapidly by investments in real estate when land could be purchased for far less per acre than it can now be bought by the square foot. Its subsequent growth is a part of the history of the growth and prosperity of the great city of New York. It was not built up, as are many railway speculative fortunes, at the expense of the loss and suffering of tens of thousands of foolish and deluded people.

The original John Jacob Astor, when asked, in his old age, if he had not too much real estate, said : "Could I begin life over again knowing what I now know and had money to invest, I would buy every foot of land on Manhattan Island."

CHAPTER XXXI.

KING BACCHUS.

NEXT to brokerage banking, probably the most profitable business places within the area of speculation are the restaurants, lunch buffets and drinking saloons. Of these Delmonico's gets the cream of patronage and takes the lead in style.

The Broadway Delmonico's for a long time adjoined the Equitable Insurance building between Pine and Cedar streets—in fact was an annex to it. In consideration of a moderate rent for the building Delmonico was to furnish meals and lunches to the tenants of rooms in the Equitable building at a less rate than to all other customers. The restaurant used the entire five stories. The rent was $20,000 a year. The bar, cuisine and waiter service probably cost more than the rent.

Another Delmonico's was, and is, three doors below the Stock Exchange, running through the block from Broad to New Streets. The rent and other expenses of this was as great as in the other. A third down-town Delmonico's is on Beaver Street.

The business done at these three restaurants was immense, and the profits correspondingly large. With first-class chefs, obsequious waiters, a splendid service, the richest liquors and rarest vintages, not to go to Delmonico's for one's lunch or tipple was to lose caste on "the Street."

The bar and lunch counters were on the first floor. If one wanted a square meal he or she could go up-stairs and have their wants attended to, to order. A porterhouse steak and fixings for one was a trifle of $1.50, and with accompaniment of wines and liquors the bill could be run up to $5 or $10. He could order soft crabs, terrapin, mushrooms or anything he wanted in its season.

The Broadway Delmonico's and the Metropolitan Bank building adjoining, on the corner of Pine Street, were torn down in 1885 to make room for the enlargement of the Equitable building.

These down-town places derived their chief patronage from the bankers, brokers and speculators during business hours. The up-town Delmonico's, at Madison Square, is famous all over the civilized world for its recherche dinners, public and private banquets.

On the death of the late Charles Delmonico there were no males of the name in the family to carry on the business. Charles Delmonico Crist, a nephew, came in possession, and thereupon procured a legal transformation of his name into

Charles C. Delmonico to retain his name for his restaurants.

There are saloons on every block, sometimes two or three adjoining each other, fitted up with splendid bars, mirrors, cut glass, and caterers to preside over free lunch side-boards, where soup, boiled ham, roast beef, baked beans, crackers and cheese are served out galore.

A bottle of beer is ten cents, a whisky, 15 to 20 cents, a pony of brandy, 20 to 25 cents, with Pomery Sec, Burgundy and the "Widow Cliquot" up in proportion.

In no other business is the strain on one's mind so tense as in speculation. Men by the hundreds go out to seek relief. In an adverse market the excitement of mind often overmasters the effect of the first few glasses of liquor. From this habit of going out to "brace up" many of these men become the hardest drinkers in the world. Women, too, brace up with bottles of beer brought by messengers.

Not all Wall Street men drink, but very many do. In the financial panic of '84 men were seen to pour out and toss off at a gulp a full half glass of undiluted brandy. Others stiff potations of the still more fiery absinthe. The next day or two the names of one or more of them would appear in the news tissues as "busted."

So great at times are the vicissitudes of the Street that men dressed in the height of fashion, with gold jewelery and sparkling diamonds, accustomed to deal in stocks by the thousand share lots, and to feed upon the fat of the land at Delmonico's, will become so impecunious, that for something to eat they will descend on the second or third-rate saloons. With a glass of beer they take their chance at the side-boards, as free lunch fiends, to gobble up as much food as would cost 15 to 20 cents at the restaurants.

Then there are basement-cellar saloons with beer and liquors at 5 and 10 cents a glass, and a free lunch table with baked beans, pickled tripe, crackers and cheese.

The following lines were published in 1820, and described the young men of the period in the then village of Brooklyn. It is no doubt to-day equally *apropos* to the pursuits and club life of the young men of the great village of New York :

"FOR THE LONG ISLAND STAR.

To the Editor,—

Dear Sir, I hope your goodness will excuse
   This humble effort of a female pen ;
And trust you can't ungallantly refuse
   To print it for those bipeds, call'd young men.

For surely, Sir, this village oft presents
   As strange anomaly as e'er was known ;
Ladies all lonely! while the dandy gents
   Sit at the porter house, or stroll the town.

Alas the age! when ladies' sparkling eyes,
   No more can charm like sparkling ale and beer ;
" O tempora!" must lovers' fragrant sighs,
   Have lesser fragrance than the fam'd segar?

No more th' inviting circle they regard,
   Where wit and beauty spread a sweet repast .
Oysters and terrapins usurp the board;
   Exalted pleasures—most refined taste!

What are the rising prospects of the land,
   When female charms no more can " wake the soul ;"
What are our hopes, when many a youthful band,
   Pay early court to pleasure's poisoning bowl ?

                          —JULIA."

CHAPTER XXXII.

WALL STREET DETECTIVES.

THE financial centres of the city are under constant watch by detectives in the employ of the Municipal Government. They are more or less fashionably dressed; wear Prince Albert coats, white high hats or derbys in Summer, black derbys or high silk hats in Winter, with shoes highly polished.

No one but the *habitues* of the Street would suspect these urbane gentlemen of having any business but to idle away their time. A couple of these gentry used to stand by the hour on the Broadway corner of Wall Street, and then saunter around to other positions, down Wall or Broad Streets, keeping a keen eye on every passer-by. They were chiefly notable for their enormous mustaches and imperials.

The detectives are supposed to know all the prominent thieves, pickpockets, sharpers and bunco steerers in the country, certainly all those whose portraits adorn the rogues' gallery. If any such appear on "the Street" the detective taps him on the shoulder and tells him to skip; or

arrests him, if caught plying his vocation, or i
wanted for a past offence.

On one occasion a most singular-looking object
dressed in baggy clothing, like a Turk, and fear
fully ragged, with an old cap on his head and lon;
unkempt hair streaming around his face, stood fo
about two hours on the Wall Street corner
Policemen, one by one, on their rounds, steppe(
up to order him to move on, but on his whisperin;
a word in their ear, they each left him and passe(
on.   He was a picture to contemplate, but unde
his rags and apparent squalor there was an aler
body and a keen, glittering eye that took in every
body.   He was a detective under cover, on the
lay for some criminal whom he alone knew.

One of the main offices of Pinkerton's Nationa
Detective Agency is just below the Stock Ex
change, on the corner of New Street and Exchang
Place.

There are a score or more of private detectiv
agencies in various parts of the city.   Some o
them follow the most infamous business unde
heaven.   If there is a plot to ruin some othe
man a detective is put on his track and evidenc
manufactured.   Does a man doubt his wife?   I
the wife jealous and suspicious of her husband
If so, one or both put a detective on the trail o
the other.   The detectives play a game of thei
own to bleed their principals as long as possible

The whole thing ends in moonshine, or in a de-
nouement that tears families asunder.

On the failure of the Marine Bank and Grant
& Ward, the " Napoleon of Finance " was placed
under the espionage of a dozen private detectives.
He was followed home at night ; a detective sat
on guard in the hall of his house ; others were on
guard all around the block. To escape over the
roofs and down a friendly scuttle was impossible.
He was followed to his office in the morning ; detectives were in the office and halls ; outside all
the approaches to the building were guarded.
No one could come in or go out except under the
surveillance of these Hawkshaws and Vidocqs until he was finally arrested.

CHAPTER XXXIII.

THE SUB-TREASURY.

THOSE chapters in this book which treat of the operations of the Treasury, Assay Office, Custom House and the National, State and Savings Banks relate only to true finance, with none of the features of speculative gambling about them.

The United States Sub-Treasury is on the second block from Broadway, at the corner of Wall and Nassau Streets, running the length of the block to Pine Street. It stands on a spot historical as the site of Federal Hall in the time of the Revolution.

Although but two stories in height, it is an imposing building, built after the Roman Doric order of architecture, of massive granite blocks, with plain cornices and entablature. It has a gable roof projecting far out over the porticos of the Wall and Pine Street fronts. The pediments are supported by eight fluted granite columns on each end. They are so immense that they were built up in sections of five pieces in each column.

The floors are of stone, the doors are iron, and the windows are protected by a grating of round steel bars an inch in diameter, making it one of the strongest and most absolutely fire-proof buildings in this country. With its constant guard of men, it is practically impregnable against robbers and mobs. Great secrecy is maintained as to its means of defense, and every precaution is taken to make it a safe depository.

The inside centre is lighted by a dome. The building was formerly used as the Custom House until 1862. All the receipts from customs, internal revenue and from sales of contraband goods sold from United States bonded warehouses are turned into the Treasury here or at Washington, whichever place may be nearest.

Besides which, many of the banks deposit their surplus of gold and silver coin in exchange for gold and silver certificates.

The transactions in money are simply enormous, and have been as high as $900,000,000 in a single year. It has had $200,000,000 of cold cash in its vaults at one time, and 900 tons of silver in one vault. It had $38,000,000 in silver dollars stored in bags at one time.

The Assistant Treasurer of the United States at New York is ex-officio a member of the Association of Clearing House Banks. In the daily clearances the debtor or creditor balances, in favor or against the Treasury, vary from a few thousands up into the millions. The average balances one way or the other are generally in the hundred thousands.

On Saturday, March 5th, 1887, the Sub-Treasurer was debtor at the Clearing House in the sum of $843,526.61, and the statement of business for that day was:

Receipts......................	$1,466,292	27
Payments	1,476,121	47
Coin Balances	133,554,447	74
Currency Balances	19,198,241	32
Coin Certificates Outstanding	18,944,886	00

The most busy time is when the pension payments are made. About 200,000 checks come in and are paid at the Sub-Treasury every December, March, June and September. In December, 1885, it was computed that the checks so paid, if placed one on top of another, would make a pile seventy-one feet high.

Called bonds for redemption have to be sent to the Secretary of the Treasury at Washington and are paid there by checks. These checks and the interest on U. S. Bond coupons are paid either in Washington or New York, as may be most convenient.

The office is splendidly managed and is no place for drones. The Assistant Treasurer, Mr. Charles J. Canda, is a gentleman of great executive ability, a thorough financier, and rules his force with a kind but firm hand. He is ably assisted by Mr. William Sherer, who has been connected with the Treasury for more than twenty years.

When Assistant Treasurer Acton's time expired and he retired to give place to Mr. Canda, the fact that a difference of but three cents existed in the balance sheet of property turned over, and that in favor of good measure, speaks volumes, and is a bright commentary upon the honesty and integrity of the working force of the office, when we consider the enormous sums of money handled.

STATUE OF WASHINGTON.

The ascent to the portico of the Treasury on the Pine Street front is two, three and four steps up from the sidewalk, according to the grade of the street. Nassau, from Pine to Wall Street, slopes downward, so that the ascent to the portico on the Wall Street front is by a flight of eighteen stone steps extending the whole width of the building.

This end of the Treasury stands partly facing the Drexel building opposite and partly looking down Broad Street.

Built in the centre of the steps of the Treasury, and rising from the level of the Wall Street sidewalk, is a base about fifteen feet square and six feet high. On the front is the inscription in letters cut into the stone :

" On this site in Federal Hall, April 30, 1789,

George Washington took the oath as first President of the United States of America."

Lying flat on top, forward of the centre of the base, is a well-preserved reddish-brown flagstone, about five feet wide by ten feet long, and on it is inscribed in chiseled letters:

" Standing on this Stone, in the balcony of Federal Hall, April 30, 1789, George Washington took the oath as first President of the United States of America."

The marble pedestal stands back of the brown flagstone on top of the base, and on one side is inscribed :

" Erected by Voluntary Subscription under the Auspices of the Chamber of Commerce of the State of New York, November 26, 1883."

The top of the pedestal is about a foot above the floor of the portico of the Treasury, and on it stands the colossal bronze statue of Washington, facing south.

The face has a reflective, benignant expression, the right arm is half outstretched, with the hand palm down and fingers pointing over towards the Stock Exchange, on Broad Street opposite, as if in deprecation.

Thrown back from the shoulders is a mantle of bronze reaching to the ankles. The statue was designed by J. Q. Adams Ward, the sculptor, and his name is on the base of the bronze, as is also

" The Henry Bonnard Bronze Manufacturing Company of New York, 1883."

THE ASSAY OFFICE.

The Assay Office adjoins the Sub-Treasury on Wall Street, separated only by an alley on which is a car track, with a hand truck to roll the crude bars of precious metal up to the door of the smelting room as it is delivered from trucks in the street.

In front it is a low, studded, white marble building two stories in height, and has nothing imposing in appearance. In the rear is a five story and basement building where the work of melting and refining is carried on.

The Treasury and Assay Office, previous to the war of the rebellion, were both in these buildings, while the present Treasury was used for a Custom House.

In 1862, owing to the enormous increase in the business of the Government on account of the war, these buildings were found inadequate. The Merchants' Exchange, further down on the opposite side of Wall Street, was purchased for $1,000,-000, and the Custom House removed there.

The Treasury was then moved into its present quarters, and a part of the Assay Office business was also transacted in the building when first occupied. But the business of the Treasury increased so fast, as the war progressed, that it soon required the entire building.

Both the Assay Office and the Treasury, which latter is a grand and noble architectural pile, are dwarfed by the tall structures, eight to ten stories in height, in the vicinity.

Quite a large force of men are required in the Assay Office—a superintendent, assistants, book-keepers, clerks, guards, and workmen in the smelt-ing and refining department.

The metal is received just as it comes from the mines. Crude. bars of silver are about fifteen inches long by four inches thick. and one of them is a good lift. It is a sight to see molten masses of gold and silver boiling and bubbling in the cru-cibles in process of refining over intensely hot fires.

Visitors are admitted at certain times and shown the processes, but must not touch things unless allowed to handle and examine the crude metal or refined gold bars. The eye of the conductor and of the employees in the room is on the visitors from the time they enter until they leave, so strict is the surveillance.

The refined gold is cast into bricks or bars, which are of all sizes in value from $500 to $5,000 and over.

On a visit the writer was shown $150,000 in gold bars on counters in the refining room, and

$38,000,000 in gold bars all in sight, in another room or vault.

When the rate of sterling exchange is up to 490½ for demand, it is profitable to export gold, and it is immaterial whether the shipments are made in coin or gold bars. When exchange is down to 484, for short, it is profitable to import gold from Europe.

To see the process of coining the refined metal into money one must go to the U. S. Mint at Philadelphia. There the gold and silver is passed through machines and rolled out into long thin strips and is cut, tempered and stamped. There also they have a museum where the coins of all countries are on exhibit under glass.

CHAPTER XXXIV.

NEW YORK CUSTOM HOUSE.

IN the great fire of 1835, which originated in Coenties Slip, and burnt through Pearl Street to its intersection with Beaver Street, the old Merchants' Exchange was destroyed, but it was the means of checking the further spread of the conflagration.

On the same site a new Merchants' Exchange was erected, which took five or six years to build, being completed in 1842. The rotunda was for years afterwards used as a board room by the stock brokers, and rang with their peculiar cries and clatter of voices.

In 1862 the Merchants' Exchange passed into the hands of the United States Government, and has ever since been used as a Custom House.

It occupies an entire block on Wall, William Streets, Exchange Place and Hanover Street. It is a massive building, built of dark Quincy granite and solid masonry, and is absolutely fire-proof.

A series of stone steps and platforms leads from Wall Street up to the rotunda on the main floor. The architrave over the entrance is supported by a colonnade of twelve fluted Ionic columns, and the ceiling by another line of four columns, with two more shafts back of them, one on either side of the main doors.

These columns are about thirty feet high, in single blocks weighing over thirty tons each, and stand on immense solid pedestals of granite. They are said to be among the largest single columns in the world. Those supporting the projecting roof over the portico of the Sub-Treasury are very much larger, but they are in sections of five pieces in each shaft.

The rotunda in the centre of the building is lighted by a magnificent dome, and had an enormous spread eagle suspended from the apex. The dome is of solid stonework and glass, and is supported by eight Corinthian columns of Italian marble over forty feet high, two on each of the four sides of the circle.

In the centre is a circular row of desks facing outward to a wide passage all around, outside of which is an outer row of desks facing inward.

The rotunda itself is a building within a building, so to speak, and outside of it are the executive offices and the Collector's rooms. Light wells afford light, air and ventilation between the inner and outer offices all through the building.

The Custom House business is enormous, and besides the great number of employees in the building, a very large force is employed outside all along the river fronts, as gaugers, warehouse-men, appraisers, accountants and examiners. Government detectives are on constant watch against smuggling. New tricks to evade payment of duties are constantly invented, trunks and valises with false sides, bottoms and pockets, diamonds concealed in the heels of shoes, and in one instance diamonds inside of a rattle tied to a baby's wrist escaped detection.

CHAPTER XXXV.

CLEARING HOUSE BANKS.

IN a former chapter the proprietors of stock houses were styled "bastard bankers." Why so? Because they deposit their money and keep their accounts at the National and State banks and pay out their money on checks the same as anybody else. Now there are two kinds of apples, the bastard Spitzenberg and the true Spitzenberg. Hence in the view of the writer the broker-banker stands in the same relation to the true banker, who is the depository and safeguard of the people's money, as the false and the true Spitzenberg stand to each other.

Business men who turn their money over and over in their frequent transactions usually keep an account and deposit their money with some bank, against which they draw their own checks in making payments to each other. These checks, when paid at the bank and returned to the drawer, are the best kind of vouchers. People who keep no bank account procure cashier's drafts for safety and convenience in transmitting money to more or less distant points.

All these checks and drafts come back into as

many different banks as there are in a large city, for payment or collection. Perhaps not one of them are paid by the bank on which they are drawn until they come around to it by due process of transfer.

Banks all over the country have their correspondent banks in New York or in other large cities, through which the drafts and checks of their customers are adjusted.

For instance, a certified check or draft, drawn on or by a bank at Omaha, Nebraska, may be sent payable to the order of a party in New York. The correspondent of the Omaha bank may be the National Broadway Bank. The party to whom the certificate is payable may keep his account with the Bank of America, and leaves the certificate there for collection. The latter must look to the National Broadway Bank to adjust it. This is done through the settlements at the Clearing House.

Under the old system of clearances, messengers had to run around all day between the various banks to exchange checks and drafts and have all differences settled. Not unfrequently the messengers had to carry large rolls of bills or bags of gold between one bank and another in settlement, at the imminent peril of being robbed on the streets.

The idea of a Clearing House system first originated with the late Albert Gallatin, President of what is now the Gallatin National Bank.

In the latter part of 1853 a Clearing House Association of over fifty banks was formed, and a new departure taken which completely revolutionized and simplified the old system of clearances.

The Clearing House, formerly at the corner of Wall and William Streets, now occupies the whole building, above the first story, at the corner of Pine and Nassau Streets, opposite the Sub-Treasury.

Imagine a long, airy, high ceiling, well lighted room, with a platform at one end for the Manager, Assistant Manager, proof and other clerks. Extending lengthwise are three long rows of double desks with wire network partitions running across the desks every three feet apart. These form separate desks, each with the name of its bank.

Each bank, of which there are about sixty-five in the Association, including the Sub-Treasury, has one Settling Clerk and one Delivery Clerk. The Settling Clerk sits at the desk of his bank to receive checks and drafts. The Delivery Clerk makes his rounds on the side opposite facing the Settling Clerks, to the desks of all the other banks with whom he has exchanges, and distributes his accounts to the Settling Clerks to be receipted for.

By a system of debit and credit tickets, each settling clerk makes up his accounts on a settling sheet, and credits or debits it opposite the name of the bank from which the exchange was received.

He then sends his debit and credit tickets to the proof clerk, at the manager's desk, to be entered on a proof sheet, which, when footed up, must make the totals balance.

In case any settling clerk makes a mistake, he must go over his work and send the result on a correction ticket back to the proof clerk, who also corrects the account on his proof sheet and makes it balance.

The manager, his assistant and clerks, and the clearing clerks of the various banks and the Treasury are in their places. Promptly at 10 o'clock A.M., the stroke of a gong brings all to attention. At a second stroke of the gong the work commences, and the business of making exchanges is done in from ten to fifteen minutes, except that the settling clerks remain to make their proofs, and ascertain the differences between their own and the other banks.

All the work is completed within an hour, and by 1:30 o'clock P.M. each bank has received or paid balances credited or debited to it, through the Clearing House, which is simply the agent to receive money from one bank to pay over to another in the adjustment of the daily differences.

On Saturdays, or if that happens to be a holiday, then on the day previous, the bank statement for the week is made up, and a few minutes after 12 o'clock, noon, the result appears on the tapes in all the brokers' offices in the city.

As the tickers reel it off, it is in form, with variation of increase or decrease, like this: Reserve Decrease, $4,086,200; Loans Increase, $1,-063,500; Specie Decrease, $4,578,400; Legal Tenders Decrease, $586,800; Deposits Decrease, $4,316,000; Circulation Decrease, $39,900.

This bank statement was for the week ending Saturday, February 26, 1887, and left the reserve in the banks at $11,398,000 in excess of the twenty-five per cent. limit required by law. February 22d was a holiday, Washington's birthday. The total business of the week of five days was;

	Totals.	Changes.
Loans......	$368,413,500	Inc. $1,063,500
Specie.......	87,068,800	Dec. 4,578,400
Legal tenders	21,189,900	" 586,800
Deposits.....	387,462,800	" 4,316,000
Circulation .	7,606,700	" 39,900

The movement of money has at times a potent influence on stock speculation, as it is a sort of barometer showing which way the financial wind is blowing. The appearance of the bank statement is eagerly watched for and the figures closely scanned.

At times immense sums of ready money are withdrawn from the banks to move the crops in the South and West, or for export to Europe.

All this will show in a decrease of the bank reserves.

In speculation one of the strongest bear arguments is the export of gold. When the bank reserve is close around the legal limit, the bears often resort to artifice to make money still more scarce, by withdrawing millions of it from the banks to lock it up in safe deposit vaults with the object of creating a money panic to depress prices of stocks, and enable them to cover their shorts at a good profit.

Previous to the panic of 1884 the bank reserve was at one time between six and seven millions below the twenty-five per cent. limit required by law.

After the panic, owing to the increasing depression and the withdrawal of capital from speculation and business enterprises, there was a steady increase in the bank reserves until in the Summer of 1885 the Clearing House banks had the enormous sum of close on to $65,000,000 in excess of the legal requirements, and a total reserve of upwards of $160,000,000 of ready capital, which went begging at from one-half of one per cent. to one and two per cent. interest per annum on call loans.

So immense was the plethora of idle capital that the mere idea of the bears having recourse to their old tactics of cornering the money market was so chimerical it was not even mentioned till the Fall and Winter of 1886-7, when the bank reserve became reduced to less than $8,000,000 above the legal limit at one time.

Since the organization of the Clearing House system in 1853 the total transactions up to the Summer of 1886, represented the stupendous figures of $777,400,000,000, which in words, seven hundred and seventy-seven billion four hundred millions of dollars. Few can grasp the immensity of such a sum.

The largest business on any one day was about $296,000,000. The smallest daily balance paid by the Clearing House to any one bank was ten cents, and the least paid to it by any bank to balance accounts was one cent.

Out of the vast sums paid on balances through the Clearing House in 33 years of its existence, it was estimated that $1,600,000,000 was paid in gold coin, weighing upwards of 3,000 tons of 2,000 pounds each, since the resumption of specie payments in 1879.

Since the issue of gold certificates by the Government, these have passed current, in place of the coin, in making the daily settlements. All the expenses of the Clearing House are paid by assessment on the banks belonging to the Association.

For the absolute perfection of this comprehensive and magnificent system of expediting a vast business with accuracy, and the least possible friction, great credit is due to the Manager, Mr. W. A. Camp, and to no one more than to the Assistant Manager, Mr. John P. Ritter.

The most profitable source of revenue to the banks are the discounts on commercial paper, which range from 4 to 6½ per cent.

Some Institutions, notably the Chemical Bank, have one or more experts to pass on the paper presented. They must be familiar with the commercial rating of the makers whose paper most frequently comes on the market. They must be able to judge if it is doubtful, good, or gilt edged, and to decide quickly whether to accept or reject it without recourse to the books of R. G Dun or Bradstreet in every case.

Time is money, and with such expedition an immense amount of the most profitable kind of business is done within banking hours.

Next to discounts, the interest on loans on stock collateral is very profitable when money is in brisk demand. The banks occupy relatively about the same positions in making loans on stocks to banker brokers, as the latter do in carrying stocks on margins for their customers. In case of danger they can demand more collateral to be put up as security, or call in their loans, or if necessary throw their stock collateral on the market to be sold.

In proportion to the amount of its capital, $300,000 divided into 3,000 shares of the par value of $100 per share, the Chemical National Bank, in point of wealth and amount of dividends it pays, overtops any other single bank in the city.

In the Summer of 1886 it had a surplus of $4,500,600, and paid 25 per cent. dividends on the par value bi-monthly. $3,200 per share was bid for its stock at one time.

In other words, its original capital increased from $300,000 to a market value of $9,600,000. The par value of its stock $100 per share increased to a market value of $3,200 per share. And it pays dividends at the rate of $600 per share per annum.

Next in wealth was the First National Bank, with a capital of $500,000—par 100—which had a surplus of $4,322,800, and paid 10 per cent. dividends per quarter. $1,050 per share was bid for it in 1886.

The American Exchange Bank and the Bank of Commerce had a capital of $5,000,000 each—par 100, with a surplus of $1,382,100 and $3,063,200 each respectively. They paid 3½ and 4 per cent. semi-annually, and their stock was quoted at 133 and 168 each per share.

It is a singular fact that most of the banks which have the least capital are the ones that make the best profits and pay the best dividends.

The Lincoln National Bank has the strongest safe deposit vaults of any bank in this country, and it is here the Vanderbilts keep their personal wealth. After W. H. Vanderbilt's death it was no small task to go over the vast number of stocks, bonds and securities in the vaults and divide them up according to the terms of his will. And in no other country probably could a family have an ex-Cabinet Minister as President of their Bank. That is what Thomas L. James, ex-Postmaster-General is.

The Savings Banks are a great blessing to people of small means. They are the conservators and promoters of economy and thrift. Without them people who could lay by only an insignificant pittance per week or month would have no incentive to be saving and to make provision for sickness and old age. The small sums turned into the Saving Banks by hundreds of the middling and poor class of people to draw interest, make an aggregate of hundreds of milions of wealth.

VISITORS' DIRECTORY.

IN AND AROUND NEW YORK.

New York is the fourth largest city on the globe. It is only exceeded in population by London, Paris and Canton. So rapid is the increase in buildings and inhabitants that two or three years hence it will probably surpass Canton and take rank as the third greatest city of the world. Its present population is estimated at 1,400,000. With Brooklyn and other cities and villages within a radius of twenty miles of the New York City Hall there are now probably about 3,000,000 of people.

Manhattan Island is a long, narrow strip of land but little more than two miles across in its widest part. It is admirably adapted to the elevated railway system it enjoys, of which it has four lines, all with a terminus at the Battery, and all, except the Ninth avenue line, running through to the Harlem River. It has numerous surface railways and is being rapidly gridironed with cross-town lines. Already the march of improvements and means of rapid transit is in the direction of underground railways and pneumatic tubes running the length of the island; the first for both passengers and freight, the last to shoot packages, messages and letters through from one point to another.

Strangers to the city cannot take in half the sights without a guide to post and direct them. The central point of direction is from the City Hall, which is about three-fourths of a mile above the extreme southern end of the island at the Battery.

City Hall Park is a triangle on the east side of Broadway. The Post Office is on the south point, back of it is the City Hall, and back of that, on Chambers Street, is the County Court House, that Tweed built. Park Row, Printing House Square, runs from the southern point of the triangle, on the east side, to Chatham Street and the New York end of the Brooklyn Bridge. Nearly all the great newspaper offices are in this vicinity.

The Astor House is on the west side of Broadway, and St. Paul's Church is on the next block south, corner of Vesey Street.

One block south of the Post Office, Fulton Street crosses the city. Fulton Market on the East River end and Washington Market on the North River side are perfect museums of meats, sea food and vegetables. The old United States Hotel is on Fulton Street, a few blocks from Fulton Ferry.

On the west side of Broadway, south to the Battery, are the tall buildings of the North British and

Mercantile Insurance Co., and the Western Union Telegraph Co. The Trinity Building and Trinity Church and churchyard occupy the whole block from Thames to Rector Streets, and Broadway to New Church Street. This is one of the most interesting places in the city and recalls many memories of by-gone generations. Here is the grave of Charlotte Temple; the tombs of Alexander Hamilton, Albert Gallatin, and Captain James Lawrence, who was killed in action between the frigates Chesapeake and Shannon. Lawrence's last words were, "Don't give up the ship." Many of the old brown tombstones are fast crumbling to decay. Parts of the graveyard are honeycombed with old vaults, and it is only at long intervals that one is opened to give sepulchre to a descendant of some old family.

On the north side near the Trinity building is the Martyrs' Monument to the memory of the men who died victims to British cruelty in the old Sugar House. It is 40 or 45 feet high, of brown stone. The base is about 15 feet square and 20 feet high, and is surmounted with a baldachin, from the roof of which rises a pinnacle capped with a stone sphere on which is an eagle with outspread wings.

The steeple of Trinity Church was formerly a great point of lookout to take a bird's-eye view of the city. It is now not much used, as visitors can ascend by elevators to the roofs of the tall buildings in the vicinity without the fatigue of climbing the steep spiral staircase.

Below Rector Street are the offices of the Adams and the American Express Companies. Near Bowling Green is the Stevens House, and the Washington Building, 11 stories high, is at the foot of Broadway, at Battery Park.

On the east side of Broadway from Fulton Street south, is the " Evening Post " Building. The Equitable Insurance Building now covers about three-fourths of the entire block on Broadway, Cedar, Pine and Nassau Streets. It was recently enlarged to more than twice its original size at a cost of probably between one and two millions of dollars, all of which, with the land, was paid for from the profits on forfeited life insurance policies. It is 8 to 9 stories high, and the hundreds of rooms rented are a most profitable source of revenue to the Equitable Company, besides those used for its own offices.

The United Bank Building, on the corner of Wall Street, is 9 stories high above the basement. It takes its name from the fact that the First National Bank and the Bank of the Republic occupy the entire first floor not used for hall room and elevators.

The Schermerhorn building is a tall, narrow structure, with as many faces as the Trimurti or triad of the Vedas. On Broadway the hall runs through to a transverse hall extending through the block from Wall to Pine Streets. It adjoins the United Bank building on the north and east.

The United States Express Company and the Consolidated Stock, Mining and Petroleum Exchange is on the next block down Broadway. Just beyond, on the corner of Exchange Place, is the Exchange Court building, belonging to the Astor family.

The new Standard Oil building, near Bowling Green, is nine stories high on Broadway and ten stories high on New Street. It towers far above its neighbors and is of vast dimensions, being $87\frac{1}{2}$ feet wide and 209 feet deep through the block. It is 165 feet from the curb to the roof, and from the foundation stone to the top of the granite work it is 190 feet. The Broadway front is of white granite, massive granite steps lead up into a vestibule of pure white Italian marble, while marble stairways climb story after story until the "outlook room" is reached. From this the view overlooking the city, Long Island, New Jersey, Staten Island, far down to the Narrows, the Brooklyn Bridge, the bay and islands in the harbor, is magnificent beyond description.

The great Welles building adjoins the last, and the Produce Exchange is across Beaver Street opposite. South of Bowling Green are the offices of the English, French and German consulates. Those of other nations are near by on State Street and Broadway.

The old Produce Exchange, on the block at
Whitehall, Water, and Pearl Streets, was purchased
by the United States Government, and a new
building is now being erected for army purposes.
Over the front entrance is the inscription, " War
1886 Department, United States Army Building."

The Battery covers an area of about 20
acres and has beautiful walks and shade trees.
Castle Garden is on the west side by the sea wall.
In the old times it was the resort of the richest
people in the city, who then lived in the vicinity.

The South and Hamilton Avenue ferries to
Brooklyn, the ferry to Bay Ridge, the Staten
Island ferries, the elevated railway terminus, the
Barge Office and the Associated Press marine
news office are all at the foot of Battery Park.

Off from Broadway, at 8, 10 and 12 Wall
Street, is the tall Astor Building running through
the block to Pine Street. Opposite, at 9 Wall
Street, is the Mortimer building. The entrance
to the gallery of the Stock Exchange is just
below at 13 Wall Street. Further down, east of
Broad Street, is the Sub-Treasury, Assay Office,
the Drexel and the great Mills buildings. The
Bank of the Manhattan Company is the most
magnificent building on Wall Street. The Custom House is the most solid and sombre. The
Cotton Exchange is around on Beaver Street, near
the Custom House, and the building formerly

occupied by the Marine Bank is corner of Wall and Pearl Streets.

On Nassau Street, corner of Pine, is the Clearing House, and one block beyond is the Mutual Life Insurance, one of the most magnificent office buildings in the city. Ex-President Arthur had his office there, and the directory in the hall read:

KNEVALS & RANSOM,
CHESTER A. ARTHUR.

Above the City Hall, corner of Broadway and Chambers Street, is the Stewart building, formerly A. T. Stewart's down town store. Chambers Street is occupied very largely by the wholesale hardware trade, while the wholesale dry goods district is between Reade and Canal Streets.

The Tombs city prison is about six blocks north of the City Hall, on Centre Street. It is an imposing building of the Egyptian order of architecture.

The Bowery is a wide busy street, a few blocks east of Broadway, running from Chatham Square to Astor Place. It is mostly occupied by Jews and Germans.

The Astor Free Library on Lafayette Place is one of the most beneficent institutions in the city. The buildings and books are valued at over $1,000,000.

Hotels are very numerous, and the best ones are mostly in the vicinity of Madison Square.

Union Square at Broadway and Fourteenth Street is a fine little park of between 3 and 4 acres. It is a nice place with a fountain and shade trees, and is surrounded by handsome buildings. It has statues of Washington, Lafayette and Lincoln.

Madison Square, the finest small park in the city, is between Broadway and Madison Avenue and Twenty-third and Twenty-sixth Streets. It is beautifully laid out with walks, shade trees, a fountain, grass and flowers. It has a bronze statute of Wm. H. Seward. Madison Square Garden is close by, occupying the entire block between Madison and Fourth Avenues and Twenty-sixth and Twenty-seventh Streets.

Gramercy Park, at Twentieth and Twenty-first Streets and Third and Fourth Avenues, is a fine place, surrounded by elegant residences.

The Cooper Union, at junction of Third Avenue and the Bowery, is a massive brown stone building, six stories high, and cost $630,000. Rooms are set apart for a free school of science and art, with a library and free reading room, which was endowed with $150,000 by the late Peter Cooper.

The Bible House is on Eighth and Ninth Streets, between Third and Fourth Avenues.

The Mercantile Library is at Clinton Hall, Astor place, and contains about 185,000 volumes. The initiation fee is $1, with a charge of $4 and $5 a year for the library privileges.

The University of the City of New York is on the east side of Washington Square.

Chickering Hall is at Fifth Avenue and West Eighteenth Street.

The College of the City of New York is corner of Twenty-third Street and Lexington Avenue.

College of Physcians and Surgeons is corner Twenty-third Street and Fourth Avenue.

Columbia College is on Forty-ninth and Fiftieth Streets, between Fourth and Madison Avenues.

New York College of Dentistry is at Twenty-third Street and Second Avenue.

The Morgue and Bellevue Hospital are near the foot of Twenty-sixth Street and East River.

The American Art Gallery is at 6 East Twenty-third Street.

The Eden Musée is on Twenty-third Street, between Fifth and Sixth Avenues.

Academy of Music, Fourteenth Street and Irving Place.

State Arsenal, Seventh Avenue and Thirty-fifth Street.

Ludlow Street Jail is on Ludlow, near Grand Street.

Jefferson Market Court and Prison, Sixth Avenue and West Tenth Street.

Institution for the Blind, Ninth Avenue, between Thirty-third and Thirty-fourth Streets.

Coal and Iron Exchange, Cortlandt and New Church Streets.

The Croton Water Distributing Reservoir is on Fifth Avenue, between Fortieth and Forty-second Streets. Just back of this is the old site of the Crystal Palace.

Lenox Library and Art Gallery, Fifth Avenue and Seventieth Street.

The Rogues' Gallery is at Police Head-quarters, 300 Mulberry Street.

There are over 400 churches in the city of various denominations.

Grace Church, at Broadway and Tenth Street, is one of the most fashionable in the city, and next to Trinity Parish, is the richest corporation of the P. E. denomination.

St. Patrick's Cathedral, Fifth Avenue, Fiftieth and Fifty-first Streets, is the most splendid church edifice in America. The height of the front gable is 156 feet, and the towers and spires, when completed, will be 330 feet in height. The building is of white marble on a base of granite. The interior appearance is as grand as the exterior. The estimated cost when completed is $2,500,000. The Cathedral is open to visitors daily. The residences of some of the greatest millionaires in the city are in the vicinity.

High Bridge Croton Aqueduct is at One Hundred and Seventy-fifth Street, Harlem River. To reach this point take Sixth Avenue elevated trains from South Ferry and intermediate stations to One Hundred and Fifty-fifth Street; thence by the Northern Railroad, one mile, to the bridge.

Fort Washington is on the Hudson River bluffs around One Hundred and Seventy-fifth Street. The earthwork and garrison of 3,000 men was captured by the British in 1776.

The New York Institution for the Deaf and Dumb, the largest school of its kind in America, is on One Hundred and Sixty-second Street, near the North River.

Of play houses of the better class there are more than a score, and many dime museums. Concert Halls are very numerous, and many of them of the most disreputable character.

A monster painting by the noted French artist, Paul Philoppotteaux, entitled "The Cyclorama of the Battles of Vicksburg," had a large run, but is soon to be removed to the West.

The fare on the elevated railroads is now five cents at all hours and for all distances. The trip to Harlem Bridge over the Third Avenue line, passing through the Bowery, is a pleasant one. This road lands passengers right at the Grand Central Depot.

The most delightful excursion inside the city is by the Sixth Avenue elevated, $9\frac{1}{2}$ miles from the Battery to One Hundred and Fifty-fifth Street, within one mile of High Bridge, all for five cents. The high trestlework above One Hundred and

Fourth Street excites admiration and wonder. The Count De Lesseps, when passing over the highest point of the road, was asked his opinion of it as a triumph of engineering. He replied sententiously, with one word : " Stupendous." In places passengers passing look over the tops of four story and basement buildings.

The Central Park extends from Fifty-ninth to One Hundred and Tenth Street, and from Fifth to Eighth Avenues, an area of about 840 acres. It is reached by Sixth Avenue elevated trains to Fifth-ninth Street and by various lines of horse cars. It has eighteen entrances, designated as the Scholars' Gate, Artists' Gate, Hunters' Gate, Mariners' Gate, Warriors' Gate, etc. It has bridges, tunnels, terraces, marble arches and fountains, lakes with pleasure boats, a carrousel, casino, rambles and carriage drives. The Mall is a grand promenade near the line of Seventy-second Street. Near this point are the statues of Columbus, Commerce, Halleck, Humboldt, hunter and dog, Mazzini, Morse, Schiller, Scott, Shakespeare, Webster, and a bronze statute in memory of the members of New York's famous Seventh Regiment who fell in battle during the civil war. The menagerie in the old Arsenal is near Fifth Avenue at Sixty-fourth Street. The Obelisk and Metropolitan Museum of Art are near Fifth Avenue at Eighty-third Street. The art gallery is full of fine paintings, many of great value. " Columbus before

Ferdinand and Isabella" cost $20,000. There are statues and reclining statues in pure white marble, one of Queen Semiramis, and one of Cleopatra and the asp ; old coins, jugs, pottery and rare unique specimens of the lares and penates of the ancients, possibly dating back to the. time of Herodotus and Homer. The great Croton Water Reservoir covers 143 acres, between Seventy-ninth and Ninety-sixth Streets.

The Brooklyn Bridge may be rightly called " the eighth wonder of the world." Its length is 5,989 feet, width 85 feet, height of towers above high water 278 feet, centre of river span is about 135 feet above high tide It has two car tracks, two roadways and a wide promenade. In the single year 1886, 24,478,324 passengers crossed over it. If all these were placed three abreast, and allowing two feet between columns, the line would reach from New York to San Francisco, and there would be people enough left over to populate a city like Brooklyn with its 800,000 inhabitants.

All tourists will wish to visit Gen. Grant's tomb at Riverside Park. This is reached by Sixth Avenue elevated trains, stopping at One Hundred and Twenty-fifth Street station.

In the Summer season the most pleasant water excursions are to Starin's Glen Island on the Sound, passing Blackwell's, Ward's, and other islands near Hell Gate. A trip up the North River to Fort Lee on the Palisades, or down the bay to Staten Island and through the Kills, is pleasant. A taste of the ocean may be had by taking boats to Coney Island and Rockaway Beach, passing between the fortifications at the Narrows. An extended ocean sail of thirty miles to Long Branch costs but 60 cents at excursion rates.

Railways radiate in all directions, conveying pleasure seekers to Coney Island and Rockaway Beach within half an hour to an hour. Others run to various resorts on Long Island, up the Hudson River, along the Sound, and to places in New Jersey.

Governor's Island, the Military Headquarters of the Department of the Atlantic, lies 1,066 yards southeast of the Battery and contains about 70 acres. On the east ridge of the island are the residences of Major-General Schofield and other officers of the post. Above the landing is the Guard House, with a squad on hand to take turns in relieving the sentinel on duty, day and night. A military museum is near by, containing a great many curiosities, not the least of which is the horse, stuffed, mounted and accoutred, that Gen. Sheridan rode " From Winchester, twenty miles away."

On the north centre of the island is Fort Columbus, an immense earthwork, inside of which are the soldiers' quarters in buildings ranged around the four sides of a square. It can mount

105 guns. South Battery commands the approaches towards that end of the island. Castle William, a round tower on the northwest end, was built in 1812. It has casemates for eighty guns, and forty can be mounted en barbette. It is sometimes used as a military prison for deserters and others. Along the north shore are to be seen immense piles of cannon balls and dismounted cannon and mortars. Ferry is run by the Government free.

Bedloe's, now called Liberty, Island, is 2,950 yards southwest from the Battery. Formerly the site of Fort Wood, it is now the resting place of the great Bartholdi statue of "Liberty Enlightening the World." The pedestal and statue is 305 feet high from foundation to top of torch. It is only exceeded in height in this country by the Washington Monument, 555 feet, and Philadelphia City Hall, 535 feet. Ferry from Barge Office at the Battery ; fare, 25 cents round trip.

Ellis, sometimes called Hangman's, Island, is north by west of Bedloe's, and is the site of Fort Gibson. Between it and the New Jersey shore is another island, with a Government storehouse and powder magazine.

In Brooklyn the chief point of interest will be the United States Navy Yard, with entrance at the York street gate. The most interesting things and places are the museum and library in the Lyceum building. The immense dry dock, built of granite, is the largest in the world, being 307 feet long by 98 feet wide, top measurement, and 286 feet long by 35 feet wide at bottom. It cost over $2,000,000. A curious rope ferry conveys visitors over to the Cob dock, where the Receiving Ship Colorado is moored. It is a sort of house, built up on the hull of a ship to a height of four or five stories, and looks like a Noah's Ark. Near by is a sailors' chapel and library, scrupulously neat. It has immense store-houses and machine shops, the Marine Barracks and Marine Hospital. Usually there is a ship of war alongside the dock refitting or taking in stores, which visitors may be allowed to inspect.

Prospect Park, Brooklyn's pleasure ground, covers between 500 and 600 acres. The site is elevated, overlooking the city, New York, the bay and ocean. It is covered with broad meadows, wooded hills and depressions, a lake, ponds and parade ground. The Ocean Parkway, a grand boulevard, 210 feet wide, runs from the Park to the Concourse at Coney Island.

Greenwood Cemetery, in the south part of Brooklyn, is one of the finest in this country. It contains 450 acres, and has many fine monuments, tombs, and a Receiving Tomb which will hold about 1,500 bodies. The interments in it number over 200,000.

Cypress Hills Cemetery, about one mile east of

Brooklyn, contains 400 acres, and is very handsomely laid out.

To get an idea of the immense commerce of the Port of New York one has only to visit the great storehouses, bonded warehouses and grain elevators along the Brooklyn water front from the Navy Yard to and up along the Gowanus Canal. The receipts from home and foreign ports, and the shipments for home consumption and export are enormous.

Brooklyn is par excellence a city of residences. It is also the "City of Churches." Plymouth Church, on Orange Street, and the Brooklyn Tabernacle, on Schermerhorn Street, have a world-wide fame. The former will seat about 2,800 persons, and the latter over 3,000.

Second only to Mr. Beecher is the fame of Rev. T. De Witt Talmage, and his audiences are only limited by the size of the Tabernacle to hold people packed like sardines. We have Talmage still.

Rev. Henry Ward Beecher's fame was so far reaching that Plymouth Church was always filled to overflowing to hear him. In New York when a stranger asked the way to Plymouth Church he was "told to cross Fulton Ferry and follow the crowd." But, alas! At the very time of this writing, Mr. Beecher's body lies cold in death, awaiting burial. The pulpit and his coffin, as his remains lie in state in the church he loved so well, are banked with flowers, while an almost endless procession are passing by for a last look. The public sorrow is universal. No man in America will be so missed as he. Who can fill the void? He was the greatest preacher and orator of his time. Take him all in all he was the greatest man this country has produced. His last words, in answer to the doctor, were: " You say I cannot get well."

www.ingramcontent.com/pod-product-compliance
Lightning Source LLC
Chambersburg PA
CBHW020850020726
47497CB00005B/1335